MW01049150

EDL Core Vocabularies in Reading, Mathematics, Science, and Social Studies

A Revised Core Vocabulary

Stanford E. Taylor
Helen Frackenpohl
Catherine E. White

Core Vocabulary for Mathematics, Grades 1-6

Betty Willmon
Nieroroda
Carole Livingston
Browning

Core Vocabularies for Science and Social Studies

E. Patricia Birsner

Foreword

EDL's purpose in developing and publishing core vocabularies is to improve the readability of instructional materials. Vocabulary load is acknowledged as the major factor in determining readability. EDL's vocabulary lists will provide teachers, authors, and researchers with word lists to be used in the writing and evaluation of instructional materials.

HISTORY
EDL's involvement in the development of core vocabularies extends over three decades.
- The reading core vocabulary dates back to 1949 with the publication of *Basic Vocabulary*[1] by the Washington Square Reading Center, EDL's parent organization. This vocabulary was subsequently revised in 1951,[2] 1955,[3] and 1969.[4]
- The mathematics core vocabulary was published in 1975.[5]
- The science and social studies lists were developed in 1978 and are now being published for the first time.

This publication brings together the reading, mathematics, science, and social studies lists into one volume. Further, it includes grade-by-grade lists for reading, a cumulative alphabetical list, and an adult word list appropriate for adults reading at low levels.

A full explanation of the origin and organization of the vocabularies is found in the Appendix.

EDL READING CORE VOCABULARY
The EDL Reading Core Vocabulary is composed of words introduced in the more widely used basal reading series and/or found on frequency lists. Its sources are described in detail in the Appendix.

There are 14 **graded** lists for levels from pre-primer through 13. Each list is arranged in alphabetical order and includes only the words introduced on the specified grade level. However, it is assumed that students already know the words contained in all of the lists for the preceding levels.

The **cumulative** list contains all of the words used in grades pre-primer through 13, arranged alphabetically, and indexed as to grade level. A number (or *P* for pre-primer) is placed before each word in this list to indicate the level at which the word is introduced.

EDL MATHEMATICS CORE VOCABULARY
The mathematics core vocabulary is based on two doctoral dissertations. The purpose of these dissertations was to compile an inventory of the frequency of use of modern mathematical terms in commonly used basal mathematics series. The availability of these word lists enables the mathematics teacher to provide instruction in mathematics terms according to their frequency and importance. One list contains words introduced in grades 1-3, a second list contains words introduced in grades 4-6.

EDL SCIENCE AND SOCIAL STUDIES CORE VOCABULARIES
The science and social studies lists are based on frequency of occurrence in glossaries of words found in the major textbook series. Since the understanding of vocabulary and concepts goes hand-in-hand in content area learning, these lists enable teachers and writers to develop vocabulary exercises with words appropriate for the various grade levels.

A science list and a social studies list are provided for each of grades 3, 4, 5, and 6.

HOW TEACHERS CAN USE THE WORD LISTS
Teachers will find a variety of uses for the word lists:

Readability levels of instructional materials can be determined. If more than 10 percent of the total vocabulary is above the student's reading level, the teacher should plan to aid the student in reading the material.

Informal inventories can be developed to assess a student's instructional level in reading or in a content area.

The student is asked to read through a graded list of words. The student should know 90 percent or more of the words on a given level in order to be considered qualified to work independently in materials written at that level.

Vocabulary improvement exercises can be based on a given word list. The teacher can create dictionary activities, sentence-writing activities, context-clue exercises, and other kinds of exercises to improve students' understanding of word meaning and usage.

The readability of teacher-made lessons can be checked against the word list for the intended instructional level of the materials. After the above-level words in a lesson have been identified, the teacher can either rewrite the lesson or pre-teach the words in question.

HOW WRITERS CAN USE THE WORD LISTS
Writers of instructional materials, childrens' stories, or trade books can use the word lists to ensure that these materials can be read independently by students in the intended target audience. (Books to be read to children by parents might be exempted from this procedure.) First, the writer must determine the grade level of the target audience. The vocabulary level of words used can be checked against the Core Vocabulary either during or after the writing of the first draft. Above-level words should be marked by circling or highlighting. Each above-level word should be considered individually. Words that are critical to the presentation of key concepts can be explained with various types of context clues (synonyms, opposites, direct explanation, etc.). Other words can be eliminated. The writer can refer to the graded lists for possible synonyms or for simpler ways of presenting the concepts.

[1] Stanford E. Taylor, *Basic Vocabulary*. New York: Washington Square Reading Center, 1949.
[2] Earl A. Taylor, Stanford E. Taylor, and Helen Frackenpohl, *Basic Vocabulary* (Second Edition). Levittown, New York: Educational Developmental Laboratories, Inc., 1951.
[3] Stanford E. Taylor and Helen Frackenpohl, *Basic Vocabulary* (Third Revision). Huntington, New York: Educational Developmental Laboratories, Inc., 1955.
[4] Stanford E. Taylor, Helen Frackenpohl, and Catherine E. White, *A Revised Core Vocabulary*. New York: Educational Developmental Laboratories, Inc., 1960, 1969.
[5] Betty Willmon Nieroroda and Carole Livingston Browning, *Core Vocabulary for Mathematics, Grades 1-6*. New York: Educational Developmental Laboratories, Inc., 1975.

ISBN 1-55855-811-X

Copyright © 1989, 1979, 1975, 1969, 1960, 1955, 1951 Steck-Vaughn Company. All rights reserved. No part of this book may be reproduced, or utilized in any form or by any means, electronic or mechanical, including photocopying, recording, or by any information storage and retrieval system, without permission in writing from the copyright owner. Requests for permission to make copies of any part of this book should be mailed to: Copyright Permissions, Steck-Vaughn Company, P.O. Box 26015, Austin, Texas 78755. Printed and bound in the United States.

Contents

EDL Reading Core Vocabulary—Adult Word List

The aural vocabulary of adults reading at very low levels is usually higher than their reading vocabulary. Therefore, if instruction is delivered through audio cassettes or teacher lecture, the following word list should be used rather than the lists that appear on pages 4-11. The number or letter which preceeds each word indicates the reading level, from Readiness through Level 3, most appropriate for the introduction of the word. Once a word is introduced, it can be used in all subsequent levels.

A

R a
2 able
R about
2 above
1 accident
1 across
2 act
3 action
2 add
3 address
3 admit
R ads
3 adult
3 adventure
2 afford
1 afraid
1 after
2 afternoon
1 again
2 against
2 age
3 agency
2 ago
3 aim
2 air
2 airport
2 aisle
R all
2 alley
3 allow
2 almost
2 alone
3 already
2 also
2 although
1 always
1 am
2 America
2 American
3 amount
1 an
3 anchor
R and
2 angry
2 animal
3 ankle
2 answer
1 any
1 anyone
1 anything
2 apartment

3 appear
3 application
3 apply
1 are
2 arm
3 army
1 around
3 arrest
3 arrive
2 arrow
1 as
3 ashamed
R ask
R at
3 ate
2 atom
3 attack
2 attention
2 attract
2 attractive
2 August
3 aunt
2 auto
1 away

B

3 baby
1 back
1 bad
1 badly
2 bag
3 baggage
3 bait
2 bake
1 ball
2 balloon
3 band
1 bank
2 bar
1 bargain
3 bark
3 barrel
1 base
1 baseball
2 basket
3 bath
3 battle
1 be
3 beach
2 bear
2 beat
2 beautiful

3 became
1 because
3 become
R bed
1 been
1 before
1 began
3 begin
2 behind
2 believe
2 bell
2 belong
3 below
2 beside
1 best
1 bet
1 better
2 between
2 bicycle
1 big
R bill
2 birds
3 birth
3 bit
3 bite
2 black
3 blank
3 blanket
3 blaze
3 bleed
3 bless
2 blew
2 block
2 blood
2 blow
3 blue
1 board
3 boast
3 boat
2 body
2 bomb
3 bone
1 book
3 booth
3 bored
2 born
2 borrow
2 boss
2 both
2 bother
3 bottom
2 bought
3 bounce

3 bowl
1 box
1 boy
2 brave
3 bread
1 break
2 breakable
3 breathe
3 brick
2 bride
3 bridge
2 bright
1 bring
2 broke
2 broken
2 brook
2 brother
2 brought
3 bucket
2 building
3 built
3 bulb
2 bullets
3 bunch
2 burn
3 burst
3 bury
R bus
3 business
2 busy
1 but
3 butter
R buy
1 by

C

2 cabin
2 cake
2 calf
1 call
3 calm
1 came
2 camera
3 camp
R can
3 cancer
3 candy
R can't
2 captain
1 car
2 card
1 care

3 carrier
2 carry
3 case
R cash
1 catch
3 cattle
2 caught
1 cause
2 cave
1 cent
3 center
3 certain
1 chair
3 challenge
3 champion
2 chance
1 change
3 charge
3 chase
3 cheap
3 cheat
R check
3 cheek
3 cheer
3 cheese
3 chew
2 chicken
3 chief
3 chest
R child
R children
3 church
3 citizen
1 city
1 class
1 clean
2 clear
3 clever
2 cliff
2 climb
3 clinic
2 clock
3 closet
2 cloth
1 clothes
3 cloud
3 club
2 coal
1 coat
2 coffee
3 coin
1 cold

3 collar
3 collect
3 college
2 color
1 come
3 comfortable
3 community
2 company
3 condition
3 control
2 cook
2 cool
3 cord
2 corn
1 corner
1 cost
3 cough
1 could
3 count
1 country
3 county
3 couple
3 courage
2 course
3 court
1 cover
2 cow
2 cowboy
2 cowgirl
3 crack
3 crackle
1 crashed
2 crazy
3 cream
3 credit
3 crew
3 crime
3 criminal
3 crop
1 cross
2 crow
3 crowd
3 cruel
2 cry
3 cup
3 curb
3 cure
3 curtain
3 customer
2 cut
3 cute

D

2 Dad
3 damage
2 dance
1 danger
3 dangerous
3 dare
2 dark
2 date
3 daughter
R day
1 dead
3 deal
2 dear
2 death
3 debt
3 decide
3 deck
2 deep
3 degree
3 delicious
3 deliver
3 dent
3 depend
3 dept.
3 desert
2 desk
3 destroy
3 detective
3 dial
3 diamond
R did
R didn't
2 die
3 difference
3 different
3 difficult
2 dig
3 diner
3 dinner
2 diploma
3 direction
1 dirt
1 dirty
3 disappoint
3 discharge
3 discover

EDL Reading Core Vocabulary—Adult Word List

3 disease
2 dish
3 disturb
3 dizzy
R do
3 dock
R doctor
1 does
2 dog
2 doll
1 dollar
1 done
1 don't
1 door
1 down
3 dozen
2 Dr.
3 drank
3 draw
3 dream
3 drew
3 drift
1 drink
1 drive
3 driven
1 drop
1 drove
3 drown
1 drug
3 drunk
3 dry
2 duck
3 due
3 dug
2 dumb
3 during
2 dust
3 duty

E

2 each
2 ear
2 early
2 earn
2 earth
3 east
1 easy
1 eat
3 edge
2 egg
2 eight
3 either
3 elbow
3 elect

3 election
2 electric
3 electricity
2 eleven
R else
3 employment
2 empty
2 end
3 enemy
2 engine
3 enjoy
1 enough
2 enter
1 escape
3 Europe
2 even
2 evening
1 ever
R every
3 except
3 excite
3 excitement
1 exit
3 expect
3 experimental
3 explain
3 extra
1 eye

F

2 fable
1 face
3 fact
3 factory
3 faint
2 fair
1 fall
1 family
3 famous
2 fan
1 far
2 farm
2 farmer
1 fast
3 fasten
3 fat
1 father
3 fault
2 fear
3 feed
1 feel
2 feet
2 fell
2 felt

3 female
2 fence
2 few
2 field
2 fifty
1 fight
3 figure
2 fill
2 final
2 finally
1 find
2 fine
3 finger
2 finish
1 fire
2 fireplace
1 first
2 fish
2 fist
1 five
1 fix
3 flag
3 flat
2 flame
3 flash
2 flew
2 floor
3 fly
2 flying
2 fog
2 fold
3 folks
2 follow
R food
2 fool
2 foot
R for
3 force
3 foreman
2 forest
R forget
R forgot
3 forgotten
3 form
2 fort
3 forty
3 forward
3 fought
2 found
2 four
3 fourth
2 fox
3 free
3 freedom
2 freeze

2 fresh
3 Friday
R friends
1 from
2 front
2 frozen
2 fruit
2 full
3 fumes
1 fun
2 fur
3 furniture
3 fuse

G

3 gain
3 gamble
1 game
2 gang
1 garbage
1 gas
2 gate
1 gave
3 general
R gets
3 ghost
2 giant
1 girl
1 give
2 given
2 glad
3 glance
2 glass
2 glove
R go
3 God
R goes
2 gold
2 gone
R good
R got
2 govern
2 government
2 grab
3 grand
2 grass
3 gravy
2 gray
2 great
2 green
2 grew
3 grocery
1 ground
3 group

2 grow
3 growl
3 guard
2 guess
3 guide
2 gun
3 guy

H

R had
2 hair
2 half
2 hall
1 hand
3 handle
R happened
1 happy
1 hard
3 hardship
1 has
2 hat
3 hatch
3 hate
R have
R he
1 head
3 heal
1 health
1 hear
2 heard
2 heart
1 heat
2 heavy
2 height
2 held
1 hello
R help
1 her
1 here
2 herself
2 hid
1 hide
2 high
2 highest
2 hill
1 him
2 himself
3 hip
2 hire
R his
1 hit
2 hold
2 hole
R home

3 honor
3 hood
3 hook
2 hop
1 hope
2 horse
R hospital
1 hot
1 hour
1 house
1 how
3 human
2 hundred
3 hung
2 hungry
2 hunt
1 hurry
1 hurt
2 husband

I

R I
2 ice
3 idea
1 if
R I'll
3 illness
1 I'm
3 imagine
3 imagination
1 important
R in
3 inches
2 Indian
3 infection
3 instead
3 insurance
3 interest
R into
3 invent
3 invention
3 inventor
R is
2 island
R isn't
R it
2 itself

J

3 jail
3 January

2 jeans
2 jet
R jobs
3 join
1 jokes
3 judge
1 jump
1 June
2 junk
1 just

K

1 keep
2 kept
2 kill
1 kind
2 king
2 kitchen
3 knee
3 kneel
1 knew
3 knife
2 knock
3 knot
R know
2 known

L

2 lady
1 land
1 landlord
2 large
1 last
2 later
1 laughed
2 laughable
3 law
2 lay
3 lead
R learn
3 least
3 leather
1 leave
2 led
1 left
2 legs
3 lemon
3 lend

EDL Reading Core Vocabulary—Adult Word List

2 lesson	2 match	**N**	3 order	2 plane	**Q**
R let	3 mate		1 other	2 plant	
R let's	3 material	1 name	3 ought	3 plate	2 queen
1 letter	3 matter	3 nation	1 our	3 platform	2 queer
3 library	R may	3 national	1 out	1 play	2 question
3 license	1 me	1 near	2 outdoors	3 pleasant	2 quick
3 lick	3 meal	3 neck	2 outfit	1 please	2 quickly
3 lie	3 mean	1 need	2 outlaws	2 plenty	1 quiet
2 life	3 meant	2 needle	1 over	3 plow	2 quit
2 lift	3 measles	2 Negro	2 overcome	3 plug	3 quite
2 light	2 meat	3 neighbor	2 overhead	2 pocket	
2 likeness	2 medal	3 neighborhood	2 own	2 point	**R**
R likes	3 medicine	3 nerve	2 owner	R poison	
3 limp	1 meet	3 nest	2 oxygen	1 police	2 raced
2 line	R men	1 never		3 policy	2 radar
2 linen	2 mess	1 new	**P**	1 policeman	3 radio
2 list	3 message	1 next		3 polio	3 rag
2 listen	2 met	2 nice	1 paid	3 polite	2 rail
1 little	3 metal	R night	2 pail	2 pond	2 railroad
1 lives	1 middle	3 nine	2 pain	2 poor	1 rain
3 load	3 midnight	3 nineteen	2 paint	2 porch	2 raise
3 loaf	2 might	R no	3 pale	3 port	1 ran
2 log	1 miles	2 nobody	2 pan	2 pot	2 rang
2 lone	2 milk	2 nod	1 paper	3 potato	3 rather
2 lonely	2 millions	2 noise	1 parents	3 pound	1 rats
1 long	2 mind	3 noon	1 park	3 powder	3 rattle
R looked	3 mine	2 nor	3 party	3 practice	2 reach
3 lose	2 minutes	2 north	2 pass	3 prairie	1 read
1 lost	3 mirror	2 nose	2 past	3 prayer	1 ready
2 loud	1 miss	R not	2 path	3 predict	2 real
1 love	3 mistake	2 note	3 pause	3 prediction	2 reason
2 low	3 moan	3 notice	3 paw	3 premium	3 receive
2 luck	3 moment	2 November	R pay	3 prepare	3 record
2 lunch	1 Monday	1 now	3 payment	2 present	3 red
3 lung	1 money	3 numb	2 peace	1 president	3 refuse
	3 monster	3 number	3 peaceful	3 pressure	3 relative
M	2 month	3 nurse	3 pen	3 pretend	3 relax
	2 moon	2 nylon	1 penny	2 pretty	3 remain
2 machine	1 more		1 people	3 prevent	1 remember
2 mad	R morning	**O**	3 permit	3 price	1 rent
2 made	1 most		3 person	3 prince	3 repair
1 mail	1 mother	3 ocean	3 pet	3 print	3 repeat
3 main	3 motor	2 o'clock	1 phone	3 prison	3 replace
1 make	3 mountain	R of	3 piano	3 private	3 reply
3 male	3 mouse	1 off	2 pick	2 prize	3 report
1 man	2 mouth	3 offer	2 picnic	2 probably	3 rescue
3 manage	1 moved	2 office	2 pictures	2 problem	3 respect
3 manner	2 movies	1 often	2 pie	3 promise	1 rest
R many	R Mr.	3 oil	2 piece	2 proud	2 return
3 map	1 Mrs.	1 old	2 pill	1 pull	3 reward
2 mark	1 much	1 on	2 pilot	3 pulse	3 rich
3 married	3 museum	2 once	1 pipes	2 punch	1 rid
3 mask	2 music	R one	1 place	3 puppy	R ride
3 master	1 must	1 only	3 plain	1 push	3 rifle
	1 my	1 open	1 plan	1 put	1 right
	2 myself	3 operator		3 puzzle	
		1 or			

2 ring
3 ripe
2 river
2 road
3 roar
2 rock
2 rocket
2 rode
2 rodeo
2 roll
2 roof
1 room
3 root
2 rope
1 round
2 rub
2 rubber
3 rug
3 ruin
3 rule
1 run
2 runway
2 rust

S

2 sad
1 safe
1 safety
R said
3 sailor
1 sales
1 salesman
3 salt
2 same
2 sameness
3 sandwich
3 sang
1 sat
1 save
1 saw
1 say
R school
3 scramble
3 screw
2 sea
2 seal
2 seat
2 second
3 secret
R see
2 seed
2 seems
2 seen

EDL Reading Core Vocabulary—Adult Word List

2 self
1 sell
2 send
3 sense
2 sent
2 sentence
2 sergeant
3 service
2 set
2 seven
3 several
3 sex
3 shadow
1 shake
3 shame
3 shape
3 sharp
1 she
2 sheep
1 she'll
3 shell
2 shines
2 ship
1 shirt
3 shock
3 shoe
2 shook
2 shoot
1 shop
2 shore
2 short
1 shot
1 should
1 shouldn't
2 shout
3 shovel
1 show
2 shut
3 shy
1 sick
2 sickness
1 side
1 sign
3 silence
3 silent
2 silk
3 silly
2 silver
3 simple
2 since
2 sing
3 sir
2 sister
1 sit
2 sixteen
3 sixty
3 skin
2 sky
3 slave
2 sled

1 sleep
3 slender
2 slept
1 slip
2 slow
2 small
1 smart
3 smash
2 smell
2 smiles
1 smoke
1 smoking
3 snake
3 sneeze
2 snow
1 so
2 soft
2 sold
2 soldier
R some
2 somebody
R something
1 son
3 song
2 soon
3 sore
2 sorry
2 sound
2 soup
2 south
2 space
3 speak
3 spear
3 special
2 speed
2 spell
1 spend
2 splinter
2 spoil
2 spoke
1 sports
2 spot
1 spring
3 spy
2 stairs
1 stand
2 star
3 stare
1 started
3 state
1 station
1 stay
3 steadily
3 steady
3 steer
2 step
2 stick
2 still
3 stir
3 stole

3 stolen
3 stomach
2 stones
2 stood
3 stool
R stop
R store
1 storm
R story
2 stove
3 straddle
2 straight
2 strange
2 strap
3 stray
1 street
2 strip
1 strong
2 stuck
3 student
2 study
3 stupid
2 subway
3 success
2 such
2 suddenly
3 suffer
3 suggest
2 suit
2 suitable
2 summer
1 sun
R supper
3 suppose
2 sure
3 surprise
3 swallow
3 swim
2 sword

T

1 table
3 tag
2 tail
1 take
2 taken
R talk
3 tall
3 tank
3 tape
3 taste
3 taught
1 taxes
1 teachers
2 team
3 tear
2 tease
3 teeth
3 telegraph

1 telephone
R tell
3 temperature
1 ten
2 tent
3 tenth
3 terrible
2 test
1 than
1 thank
R that
R the
3 theatre
1 their
R them
3 themselves
R then
1 there
1 these
R they
2 thin
R thing
1 think
1 third
3 thirsty
2 thirty
1 this
3 thorn
1 those
2 though
R thought
3 thousand
3 threaten
2 three
3 threw
3 throat
3 through
3 throw
3 thumb
3 thunder
2 ticket
2 tie
3 tight
R time
3 tip
2 tired
R to
R today
2 toe
1 together
R told
2 tomorrow
3 tone
3 tongue
1 too
1 took
3 tool
2 tooth
2 top
3 torn

2 touch
3 tough
3 tow
2 toward
3 tower
3 town
2 toy
2 track
2 train
3 travel
3 treat
3 tree
2 trick
2 trip
1 trouble
1 truck
2 true
3 trust
3 truth
1 trying
3 tune
1 turn
2 twelve
2 twenty
1 two

U

3 unable
1 under
3 understand
3 unemployed
3 unhappy
2 United States
2 unlucky
2 unsafe
2 until
1 up
2 upstairs
3 upward
3 urge
1 us
1 use
2 useful
2 useless
3 usually

V

3 vacation
3 vegetable
3 vehicle
1 very
2 village
2 visit
3 visitor
2 voice
2 volunteer
3 vote

W

3 wag
3 wagged
3 wagon
R wait
3 waitress
2 wake
R walks
2 wall
3 wander
R wanted
2 war
2 warehouse
2 warm
3 warn
R was
2 wash
R wasn't
3 waste
1 watch
1 water
2 wave
1 way
1 we
2 wear
2 weather
3 weeding
1 week
3 weigh
3 weight
3 welcome
1 well
R went
1 we're
1 were
1 weren't
2 west
3 western
3 wet
R what
3 wheat
2 wheel
R when
R where
3 whether
1 which
2 while
3 white
1 who
2 whole
3 whose
1 why
2 wide
2 wife
2 wild
R will
1 win
2 wind
1 window

3 wine
2 winter
1 word
3 wore
R working
2 world
1 worry
2 worse
3 worst
2 worth
2 worthless
2 worthwhile
1 would
1 wouldn't
3 wound
3 wreck
3 wipe
3 wire
3 wise
2 wish
1 with
3 woke
2 wolf
2 woman
R women
2 won
1 wonder
2 wonderful
1 won't
2 wood
3 wrist
1 write
3 written
1 wrong
3 wrote

X

3 x-ray

Y

3 yard
1 year
2 yell
3 yellow
R yes 1
2 yesterday
3 yet
R you
1 young
1 your
2 yourself

Z

3 zone
2 zoo

Reading Pre-Primer

A
a
airplane
and
at
away

B
ball
big
blue

C
can
car
come

D
daddy
did
do
down

F
fast
father
for
fun
funny

G
get
go
good
green

H
have
he
help
here
home
house

I
I
in
is
it

J
jump

L
like
little
look

M
make
may
me
mother
my

N
not
now

O
on

P
play

R
red
ride
run

S
said
see
something
stop

T
the
this
to
toy
two

U
up

W
want
we
what
will
with
work

Y
yes
you

EDL Reading Core Vocabulary—Graded Lists

Reading—1

A
about
after
again
all
alone
along
am
an
animal
another
any
apple
are
around
as
ask
asked
aunt

B
baby
back
bag
balloon
barn
basket
be
bear
bed
bee
before
began
behind
being
best
better
bird
birthday
black
boat
book
box
boy
bring
brown
bus
but
buy
by

C
cake
calf
call
called

came
can't
cat
catch
children
circus
clown
coat
cold
color
coming
cookie
could
cow
cry

D
dark
day
does
dog
doing
doll
don't
door
dress
duck

E
each
eat
egg
every

F
far
farm
faster
feet
find
fine
fire
fireman
first
fish
fit
five
flew
flower
fly
found
four
friend
frog
from

G
game
garden
gave
girl
give
glad
goat
going
gone
good-by
got
grass
ground
grow
guess

H
had
hand
happy
hard
has
hat
head
hear
heard
hello
hen
her
high
hill
him
his
hold
honey
horse
hot
how
hurry

I
ice
ice cream
if
into

J just

K kitten
know

L
lamb
last
laugh
let
let's
letter
light
live
living
long
looked
lost
lunch

M
made
man
many
men
met
milk
miss
Miss
money
monkey
more
morning
Mr.
Mrs.
much
must

N
name
near
nest
never
new
next
night
no
noise
nose
nothing

O
of
off
oh
old
once
one
or
other
our

_____ **EDL Reading Core Vocabulary—Graded Lists** _____

out
over
paint

P painted
painter
painting
parade
park
party
peanut
penny
people
pet
picnic
picture
pig
please
pocket
pony
pretty
prize
pull
puppy
put

R rabbit
rain
ran
read
ready
right
road
room
running

S sang
sat
saw
school
she
shoe
shoes
show
sing
sit
sitting
sleep
snow
so
some
sometimes

soon
spring
squirrel
stay
step
stopped
store
story
street
sun
surprise

T tail
take
talk
tell
than
thank
that
their
them
then
there
these
they
thing
think
those
three
time
told
too
took
town
train
tree
trick
truck
try
turtle
twin

U uncle
under
us

V very

W wagon
walk
walked

was
water
way
went
were
wet
when
where
white
who
why
window
wish
without
woman
word
would

Y yard
year
yellow
your

Z zoo

EDL Reading Core Vocabulary—Graded Lists

Reading—2

A
able
above
across
afraid
afternoon
ago
ahead
air
almost
always
angry
answer
anyone
anything
apartment
arm
asleep
ate

B
babies
bad
bake
band
bang
bank
bark
basketball
bat
beautiful
because
been
begin
beginning
believe
bell
belong
berry
beside
between
bicycle
bigger
biggest
bill
bit
bite
blew
block
blow
board
bone
both
bottle
bottom
bought
bought

bounce
branch
brave
bread
break
breakfast
bridge
bright
broken
brother
build
building
burn
bush
busy
butter
button

C
cage
camp
candle
candy
cannot
cap
card
care
careful
carried
carry
caught
cent
chair
change
chase
chicken
chimney
chip
chipmunk
Christmas
city
clean
clever
climb
clock
close
clothes
coal
cook
corn
corner
couldn't
count
country
cover
crawl
cream
cried
cross
crow

cut
cutting

D
dad
dance
dear
deep
deer
didn't
different
dig
dinner
dirty
dish
dollar
done
donkey
drink
drive
driver
drop
drown

E
ear
early
easy
edge
eight
elephant
elevator
else
empty
end
engine
enough
even
evening
ever
everyone
everything
everywhere
excite
eye

F
face
fair
fairy
fall
family
farmer
farther
fat
feather
feed
feel
fell
felt

fence
few
field
fight
fill
finish
fix
flag
flash
flashlight
floor
flour
follow
food
foot
football
fourth
fox
friendly
frighten
front
fruit
full

G
gate
glass
glove
goes
gold
goose
grandfather
grandmother
gray
great
grew
grin

H
hair
happen
hardly
haven't
hay
heavy
held
herself
hide
himself
hit
hole
hop
hope
horn
hungry
hunt
hunter
hurt

I
idea
I'll
I'm
important
Indian
inside
isn't
its
it's
I've

J
join
joke
jolly

K
keep
kept
key
kick
kill
kind
king
kitchen
kite
knew
knock

L
ladder
lady
lake
land
large
larger
late
later
lay
leave
leaves
left
leg
library
life
line
lion
listen
lock
lot
loud
love
low
lucky

M
machine
magic

EDL Reading Core Vocabulary—Graded Lists

mail
making
mate
maybe
mean
merry
middle
might
mill
minute
moon
most
mountain
mouse
mouth
move
mud
myself

N
nail
neck
need
neighbor
nice
nine
number
nut

O
oak
o'clock
office
older
only
open
orange
outside
oven
owl
own

P
pail
pair
pan
paper
part
pass
past
pat
paw
pay
peep
pennies
pick
pie
piece
pile

pink
pipe
place
plant
point
policeman
pond
poor
pop
popcorn
present
princess
print
proud
puddle
puppet
push

Q
quack
question
quick
quickly
quiet

R
raccoon
race
radio
rag
railroad
ranch
reach
real
really
remember
rest
return
riding
ring
river
roar
rock
rode
roll
roof
rope
round
row
rub

S
sad
safe
same
Saturday
say
sea
seat
second

secret
seed
seem
seen
sell
send
sent
set
seven
shall
sheep
shiny
shook
shop
short
should
shout
shovel
shut
side
sign
silly
silver
sister
six
skate
sky
sled
slow
slowly
small
smell
smile
snowstorm
soft
someone
song
sorry
sound
soup
splash
stairs
stand
start
station
stick
still
stone
stood
stories
storm
straight
strange
string
strong
stuck
subway
such
suddenly
suit
summer

supper
suppose
sure
swim
swing
swish

T
table
tag
taken
tall
teach
teacher
tease
telephone
television
ten
tent
terrible
third
thought
threw
through
throw
ticket
tie
tiny
tired
today
together
tomorrow
tonight
toot
tooth
top
track
tractor
tried
trip
trouble
true
trunk
turn
twelve

U
unhappy
until
use
useful

V
village
visit
voice

W
wag
wait
warm

wash
wasn't
watch
wave
wear
week
weigh
well
we'll
whale
wheel
which
while
whisper
whistle
wide
wife
wild
win
wind
wing
winter
wise
woke
wolf
wonder
wonderful
won't
wood
world
write
wrong

Y
you'll
young
yourself

EDL Reading Core Vocabulary—Graded Lists

Reading—3

A
aboard
act
add
address
adventure
against
age
aim
airport
alarm
alike
alive
allow
already
also
amaze
America
American
among
amuse
announce
ant
apart
appear
April
apron
aren't
army
arrange
arrive
arrow
astonish
attack
automobile
autumn
average
awake
awful
ax

B
baggage
bait
banana
bar
bargain
barrel
base
baseball
bath
batter
beach
bead
bean
beard
beast
beat

beauty
beaver
became
become
bedroom
beehive
beg
begun
behave
below
belt
bench
bend
bent
beyond
birth
blade
blanket
blast
bless
blessing
blind
blood
blossom
blueberry
boast
body
boil
bold
boot
born
borrow
bother
bow
bowl
breath
breeze
brick
broke
brook
brush
bubble
bucket
buffalo
bug
built
bulb
bull
bunch
bundle
bunk
butcher
butterfly

C
cabin
calendar
calm
camera
canary

cannon
canoe
captain
cardboard
careless
carol
carpet
carrot
cart
carve
case
cattle
cause
cave
cellar
center
certain
certainly
chain
chance
charge
chatter
cheek
cheer
cheese
cherry
chest
chew
chick
chief
child
chin
chocolate
choose
chop
chose
chuckle
church
circle
clap
class
clear
cliff
clip
closet
cloth
clothing
cloud
club
coach
coast
coconut
coffee
colt
comb
comfortable
common
company
complain
complete

conductor
content
contest
continue
cool
copper
copy
correct
cost
costume
courage
course
cousin
coward
cozy
crack
crash
creek
crept
crowd
crown
cup
curious
curl
curtain

D
damp
danger
dare
darkness
dash
daughter
dawn
dead
decide
deck
delicious
delight
depend
desert
deserve
desk
diamond
die
difference
dime
dine
dip
direction
dirt
disappear
disappoint
discover
dive
divide
doctor
doesn't
downstairs
Dr.

drag
drank
draw
drawer
dream
drew
dried
drift
drip
drove
drum
dry
dug
dumb
during
dust

E
eager
eagle
earn
earth
easily
east
eighty
either
eleven
elf
elves
English
enjoy
enter
escape
event
everybody
exactly
example
except
excitement
exciting
exclaim
excuse
exercise
expect
explain
extra

F
fail
faint
faithful
famous
fan
fancy
fasten
fault
fear
feast
February
fed

_____ **EDL Reading Core Vocabulary—Graded Lists** _____

fellow
fiddle
fierce
fifteen
fifth
fifty
finally
finger
fisherman
flame
flap
flat
float
flow
fog
fold
fool
foolish
force
forest
forget
forgive
forgot
forgotten
form
forth
fortune
forty
forward
fourteen
frame
free
freeze
fresh
Friday
frown
fur

G
garage
gas
gather
gay
gaze
gentle
giant
gift
given
glance
glitter
gnaw
goodness
grab
grain
grease
greedy
group
growl
grown

guard
guide
gun

H
half
hall
hammer
handle
hang
happiness
harbor
harm
harness
hasn't
hate
having
hawk
healthy
heart
heat
heaven
heel
helper
helping
herd
hero
hid
hidden
highway
history
hive
holiday
hollow
honor
hoof
hook
hoop
hose
hospital
hound
hour
hug
huge
hundred
hung
husband

I
I'd
ill
imagine
impossible
inch
indeed
inn
inquire
insect
instead
intend

interest
interesting
invite
iron
island
itself

J
jar
jelly
jerk
jet
jewel
job
journey
joy
judge
juice
July
June

K
kangaroo
keeper
kiss
knife
knight
known

L
laid
lap
law
lazy
lead
leaf
leak
lean
learn
led
less
lesson
lie
lift
list
lively
load
loft
log
lonely
loose
lose
lovely
lower
lumber
lump
lying

M
mad
main

manage
map
march
mark
market
marry
master
match
matter
mayor
meadow
meal
meant
meat
meet
melt
message
metal
mice
mile
mind
mine
mirror
mischief
mistake
mix
moan
model
moment
Monday
month
motor
mount

N
nap
narrow
nation
neat
necklace
needle
neither
net
nibble
nickel
ninety
nobody
nod
none
north
note
notice
November

O
ocean
offer
often
oil
order

organ
ought
outdoors

P
pack
package
page
paid
palace
pale
parent
passenger
paste
patch
path
pea
peddler
peek
pen
pencil
perhaps
piano
pillow
pilot
pin
pine
pitch
pitcher
plain
plan
plane
planned
plate
pleasant
plenty
plow
poke
pole
police
polite
pool
porch
possible
post
pot
potato
pound
pour
power
practice
prepare
president
press
pretend
price
probably
promise
prove
puff

EDL Reading Core Vocabulary—Graded Lists

purple
puzzle

Q queen
quite

R rack
raise
rang
rapidly
rather
rattle
rear
reason
receive
recognize
record
refuse
remain
repair
repeat
replied
reply
rescue
respect
reward
rib
ribbon
rice
rich
rid
ripe
roast
robber
robe
rooster
root
rose
route
rubber
rule
ruler
rush

S safely
safety
sail
sailor
sale
salt
sand
sandwich
sank
satisfy
save
saving
scarce

scare
scarf
scatter
scene
scent
scratch
scream
search
season
seize
selfish
sense
serious
serve
seventy
several
shade
shadow
shake
shape
share
sharp
shed
sheet
shelf
shell
shine
ship
shirt
shoot
shore
shot
shy
sick
sidewalk
sigh
signal
silent
simple
since
single
sir
sixteen
sixty
size
skin
skip
slap
sleepy
sleigh
slept
slide
slip
smart
smoke
smooth
snake
snap
soap
sock
softly

sold
somebody
somehow
somewhere
son
sort
south
space
spare
spark
sparkle
speak
special
speed
spend
spider
spill
spin
spirit
split
spoil
spoke
spoon
spot
spray
spread
squeak
squeeze
stage
stamp
star
stare
startle
state
steal
steam
steep
steer
stem
stiff
sting
stir
stout
straw
stray
stream
stretch
strike
strip
struck
struggle
study
stuff
stump
stupid
sudden
Sunday
swallow
swam
sweep
sweet

swift
switch

T tank
tap
taste
taught
team
teeth
temper
tender
test
themselves
thick
thief
thin
thirsty
thirteen
thirty
though
thousand
thread
throat
Thursday
tight
till
tip
tire
toast
tool
toss
touch
toward
tower
trade
traffic
trail
trap
travel
treasure
tremble
tribe
trot
trousers
trust
truth
tube
tumble
tune
tunnel
twenty
twice

U ugly
understand
understood
unite

United States
unless
unusual
upon
upstairs
usual
usually

V vacation
valley
vegetable
visitor

W wake
wall
wander
war
warn
waste
weak
weather
weep
weight
welcome
we're
weren't
west
we've
wheat
whip
whole
whose
willing
wink
wipe
wire
wisdom
women
won
wool
wore
worm
worn
worry
worse
worth
wouldn't
wrap
wreck
written
wrote

Y yet
you're
you've

EDL Reading Core Vocabulary—Graded Lists

Reading—4

A
accent
accept
accident
according
accuse
ache
acorn
acre
acrobat
action
actor
actually
adjust
admire
admit
afford
agree
alligator
alphabet
although
altogether
amount
ancestor
anchor
ancient
anger
anxious
anybody
anyhow
appearance
approach
aquarium
area
argue
arithmetic
arrangement
arrest
article
artist
ashamed
ashes
astronaut
attention
attic
August
avenue
avoid
awkward
awoke
aye

B
bacon
badge
balance
bamboo
bandage
banner
bare
basement
bathroom
bathtub
battery
battle
bay
beak
beam
beef
beetle
bellows
beneath
bet
bid
bike
billow
birch
blame
blaze
bleat
blend
blink
blizzard
blubber
bob
bonnet
bound
bracelet
braid
brain
brass
breathe
broom
brownie
bruise
buck
buckle
buggy
bulge
bullet
bun
burro
burrow
burst
bury
bushel
business

C
cabbage
cable
calves
cane
canvas
canyon
capture
cargo
carnival
carpenter
carriage
cast
castle
celebrate
champion
character
charcoal
check
cheerful
chimpanzee
china
choke
chore
chosen
churn
citizen
claim
clam
clatter
claw
clay
climate
clover
clump
coax
cobbler
cocoa
coin
collar
collect
collection
colonel
colony
comfort
command
committee
companion
condition
cone
contain
continent
control
convenience
convenient
coral
cord
cork
corral
cot
cottage
cotton
council
counter
couple
court
cove
coyote
crab
crag
crayon
crazy
creak
creature
creep
crew
crib
cricket
cripple
crisp
crocodile
crooked
crop
crouch
cruel
crumb
cub
cupboard
cure
curiosity
curly
current
curve
custom
customer
cute

D
dairy
daisy
damage
dandy
dangerous
dangle
date
deal
death
debt
December
declare
decorate
deed
defend
degree
deliver
delivery
demand
den
department
design
dessert
destroy
detective
develop
dictionary
difficult
dignity
dim
dinosaur
direct
disappointment
discovery
disease
disgrace
disgust
dismay
distance
distant
disturb
dock
doe
doubt
dozen
dragon
drawn
dreadful
droop
dull
duty

E
earnest
earthquake
Easter
eastern
echo
editor
effect
eighteen
eighth
electric
electricity
elegant
encourage
encyclopedia
endurance
enemy
engineer
enormous
entire
envelope
equal
equator
Eskimo
especially
eve
examination
examine
exchange
expensive
experience
experiment
expert
explanation
explode
explore
express
eyebrow
eyelash
eyelid

F
fact
factory

_____ **EDL Reading Core Vocabulary—Graded Lists** _____

fade
familiar
faucet
favor
favorite
fiery
figure
fin
final
firm
fist
flare
flavor
flicker
flight
flint
flock
flood
flute
flutter
folk
fond
forehead
forever
fork
fort
fortunate
fought
freckle
freedom
freight
friendship
frontier
frozen
fry
furnace
furniture
further
fuss
future

G gallon
gallop
gang
garbage
gasp
geese
general
gentleman
ghost
giggle
giraffe
glare
gleam
glide
glisten
gloomy
glossary
glow

gobble
god
golden
gourd
government
grade
gradually
grand
grape
grasp
grateful
gravy
graze
greet
grind
grip
groan
groceries
grocery
grumble
grunt
guest
guitar
gull
gypsy

H habit
hadn't
Halloween
halt
handkerchief
handsome
harvest
hatch
health
heap
hearth
helpful
hesitate
hind
hinge
hire
hitch
hoarse
hobby
hog
honest
honesty
honk
horrify
hotel
however
howl
human
hump
hunger
hurricane
husky
hut

I icy
imagination
imitate
immediately
impatient
improve
improvement
information
ink
inning
insist
instant
instrument
interrupt
introduce
invent
invention

J jacket
jail
jam
janitor
January
jaw
jealous
jeep
jingle
Jr.
jungle

K kayak
kettle
kid
kingdom
knee
knit
knives
knot
knowledge

L lad
lame
lamp
landlord
lane
language
lantern
laughter
lawn
league
leap
least
leather
ledge
legend

lemon
lemonade
length
lettuce
level
lever
lick
lid
lightning
lime
limp
link
lip
lit
locate
locomotive
lodge
lonesome
lord
luck

M magazine
magician
magnet
maid
mama
mane
manner
manners
marble
mare
married
marsh
mast
material
mattress
meanwhile
measure
medal
medicine
mention
mesa
messenger
midnight
million
minstrel
mist
mistress
mitten
mixture
moccasin
modern
mood
moose
mop
moss
motion
mound
movies

mug
mule
mumble
murmur
museum
music
musician
musket
mustache
mutter
mysterious
mystery
myth

N national
natural
nature
naughty
navy
necessary
neighborhood
nephew
nervous
news
newspaper
nineteen
ninth
nonsense
noon
nor
northern
nuisance
nurse

O oar
oasis
oatmeal
oats
obey
object
October
officer
onion
opinion
opossum
opposite
orbit
orchard
ordinary
ornament
overhead
owe
ox

P pad
paddle
pain
palm

EDL Reading Core Vocabulary—Graded Lists

pant	pray	pit	quit	scoop
pants	prayer	pity	quiver	scooter
papa	precious	planet		score
parachute	preparation	platform		scout
paragraph	preserve	playful	**R** racket	scowl
parrot	prick	playground	rage	scramble
particular	pride	playmate	ragged	screech
partner	prince	plug	rake	screen
pasture	prison	plum	range	scythe
patient	prisoner	plunge	rare	seal
pattern	private	poison	rat	seaport
pause	problem	polar	realize	self
peace	professor	polish	refrigerator	sentence
peaceful	program	poppy	regular	September
peach	pronounce	popular	reindeer	servant
pear	proof	port	reins	service
pearl	property	porter	relief	setting
pedal	protect	position	remind	settle
peel	protection	possession	remove	settler
pepper	ornament	possibly	rent	seventeen
perfect	overhead	postman	report	seventh
perform	owe	pottery	represent	sew
period	ox	powder	reservation	shallow
permission	pad	prairie	responsible	shark
person	paddle	praise	result	shawl
persuade	pain	prance	retreat	shelter
phone	palm	pray	riddle	shepherd
pigeon	pant	prayer	ridge	sheriff
pilgrim	pants	precious	rifle	shift
pillar	papa	preparation	rim	shiver
pinch	parachute	preserve	rise	shone
pinto	paragraph	prick	roam	shoulder
pioneer	parrot	pride	rob	shove
pirate	particular	prince	robin	shower
pit	partner	prison	rocket	shreik
pity	pasture	prisoner	rodeo	shrug
planet	patient	private	rough	sight
platform	pattern	problem	royal	silence
playful	pause	professor	ruby	silk
playground	peace	program	rude	sill
playmate	peaceful	pronounce	rug	sink
plug	peach	proof	ruin	siren
plum	pear	property	rumble	sixth
plunge	pearl	protect	rustle	ski
poison	pedal	protection		skill
polar	peel	protest		skim
polish	pepper	pump	**S** sack	skirt
poppy	perfect	pumpkin	saddle	skunk
popular	perform	punish	sake	slam
port	period	pup	salad	slant
porter	permission	pupil	salute	sleeve
position	person	purpose	sauce	slender
possession	persuade		sausage	slid
possibly	phone		savage	slipper
postman	pigeon	**Q** quarrel	scale	slippery
pottery	pilgrim	quart	scamper	slope
powder	pillar	quarter	scenery	snarl
prairie	pinch	queer	scientist	sneak
praise	pinto	quill	scissors	sneeze
prance	pioneer	quilt	scold	sniff
	pirate			

EDL Reading Core Vocabulary—Graded Lists

snort
soak
soar
soldier
solve
somersault
somewhat
sore
sour
southern
spank
spear
speck
spectacle
speech
spell
spelling
spent
spike
spine
spool
sport
sprang
spy
square
squat
squawk
squeal
Sr.
stable
stack
stagger
stake
stalk
stall
stallion
stampede
starve
statement
statue
steadily
steady
steel
stern
stockade
stocking
stole
stolen
stomach
stool
stove
strain
stranger
strap
streak
strength
stride
stripe
stroke
stumble

succeed
success
suffer
sugar
suggest
suitcase
sum
sung
supplies
supply
support
surface
surrender
surround
suspect
swamp
swan
swarm
sweater
swell
swept
swoop
sword
swung
syllable

T tailor
tale
tame
tan
tangle
tape
tar
target
tea
tear
telescope
temperature
tenth
tepee
terror
thankful
Thanksgiving
therefore
thorn
threaten
thrift
thrifty
thrill
throne
thumb
thump
thunder
tide
tiger
tile
tilt
tin
toad

toe
tomato
ton
tongue
toothpaste
tore
touchdown
tough
towel
trailer
tramp
transfer
tray
treat
treaty
trim
tropical
trout
trudge
trumpet
tub
tuck
Tuesday
tug
turkey
turnip
twelfth
twinkle
twist
type
typewriter

U umbrella
umpire
uneasy
unicorn
uniform
unit
upset
urge

V valentine
vanish
vase
velvet
victory
view
vine
volcano
voyage

W waddle
wail
waist
walrus
wand

warrior
watermelon
weary
weave
web
Wednesday
wee
weed
western
wharf
wheelbarrow
whether
whine
whirl
whiskers
whittle
whom
wicked
wig
wiggle
wigwam
wilderness
willow
wine
witch
wizard
wobble
woodpecker
worst
wound
wrinkle
wrist

Y yawn
yell
yesterday

Z zero
zone

16

EDL Reading Core Vocabulary—Graded Lists

Reading—5

A
abandon
ability
absent
absorb
academy
accompany
account
accounting
achieve
achievement
adapt
addition
admiral
admiration
admission
adobe
adopt
advance
advantage
advice
advise
affect
afterward
agent
agriculture
aid
aisle
alcohol
alley
alter
altitude
aluminum
A.M.
ammunition
angel
angle
ankle
antelope
antenna
anvil
ape
apologize
appeal
appetite
appreciate
appreciation
apprentice
apricot
arch
arctic
armor
art
astonishment
astound
athletic
atmosphere
attach
attempt
attend
attendance
attract
audience
auditorium
autograph
automatic
award
aware

B
bacteria
balcony
bale
bandit
banjo
barley
barter
basin
bathe
beets
behavior
benefit
berth
bewilder
Bible
bin
bind
bitter
blank
blister
blond
bloom
bluff
blunder
blur
blush
bog
bolt
bomb
bonfire
bookkeeper
booth
border
bore
boss
bough
boulder
bouquet
brace
brag
brake
brand
breeches
breed
bride
bridle
brilliant
brisk
broad
bronze
bud
budge
bugle
bully
buoy
burden
burglar
burnt
bustle
butt

C
cab
cabinet
cactus
cafe
cafeteria
camel
canal
cape
capital
capitol
capsule
captive
caravan
cask
casual
cautious
cedar
ceiling
celebration
cell
cement
central
century
cereal
ceremony
certificate
chalk
challenge
chamber
channel
chant
chaos
chapter
charm
chart
cheap
cheat
checker
chemical
chemistry
chill
chilly
chisel
choice
choir
chorus
chum
chunk
cinder
civil
civilized
clench
clerk
cling
cloak
clue
clumsy
clung
cluster
clutch
coarse
cocoon
code
coil
college
collie
colonial
colonist
column
comment
community
compact
compare
compass
compliment
composition
comrade
concentrate
concern
concert
concrete
condense
confess
confide
confidence
confident
confuse
congratulate
congress
connect
conquer
conscious
consent
consider
construct
construction
consult
convention
conversation
convince
cooperate
correction
cough
county
crackle
cradle
craft
cranberry
crane
crank
crater
credit
crest
crime
crude
crumble
crush
crust
crystal
curb
custard

D
daily
dainty
dam
darling
darn
dart
dazzle
deaf
deafen
decision
declaration
decrease
decree
defeat
delay
delicate
demonstrate
dense
dent
dentist
deny
depot
descend
descendant
describe
desire
desperate
detail
determine
device
dew
dial
diesel
dike
diphtheria
disaster
discuss
disguise
dismiss
dispose
distress
district

ditch
division
dizzy
dodge
dogie
dominoes
dot
double
dough
doughnut
dove
drain
dread
dreary
dresser
drill
drought
drowsy
drunk
due
dues
duke
dump
dune
dusk
dwarf
dye
dynamite

E
ease
easel
educate
education
effort
elbow
elect
election
electronic
elm
embarrass
embroider
emergency
emperor
enamel
enclose
enterprise
entertain
entertainment
entirely
entrance
envy
equip
equipment
erase
eraser
errand
establish
evidence
evil

excellent
exhaust
exhausted
exhaustion
exhibit
exhibition
expedition
explosion
export
expression
extend

F
fabulous
failure
faith
fame
fare
farewell
fashion
fawn
female
fern
ferry
fertile
fertilizer
festival
fever
fiber
fig
file
fiord
flake
flee
fleet
flesh
fling
flip
floe
flop
flown
fluff
flung
foam
foreign
forge
foster
fountain
fraction
frantic
fright
frost
froze
fuel
funeral
furious
furnish
furrow
fury

G
gain
gale
galleon
gander
gap
gape
garment
gasoline
gauze
gear
generally
generation
generous
geography
germ
gin
glacier
glee
glider
glimpse
globe
glorious
glory
glue
goal
goblin
goddess
golf
gorge
governor
gown
grace
graceful
grammar
granite
grant
gratitude
grave
gravel
gravity
griddle
grim
grit
growth
gruff
guinea
gulp
gum
gust
gym

H
hail
halter
ham
hamburger
hammock
hardship

hare
harp
harpoon
hasty
haul
haunt
haze
heal
height
helicopter
helmet
herb
heron
hickory
hike
hip
hiss
hockey
hoe
hogan
holly
holy
homestead
horizon
horrible
horror
hover
huddle
hull
hum
humble
humor
humorous
hurdle
hurl
hush
hustle
hygiene
hymn

I
iceberg
idle
igloo
ignore
imaginary
immense
import
incline
include
increase
independence
index
indignant
inhabitant
innocent
inspect
instruct
instruction
intelligence

intelligent
intent
interpret
interval
inventor
invisible
invitation
iodine
irrigate
irrigation
itch
ivory

J
jewelry
jiggle
jog
journal
jug
junction
junior
junk
justice
jut

K
keen
kernel
kerosene
kindergarten
kindness
kit
kneel
knelt
knob

L
labor
laboratory
lack
lair
launch
lava
lawyer
leash
lend
lent
liberty
librarian
license
lily
limb
limestone
limit
linen
liner
lint
liquid
lizard

EDL Reading Core Vocabulary—Graded Lists

llama
loaf
loan
loaves
loom
loss
loyal
lung
lunge
lurch

M
machinery
madam
magnify
majesty
male
mammoth
mantel
manufacture
maple
mar
marvel
marvelous
mascot
mash
mask
mass
mat
meek
melody
member
memorial
memory
mend
merchant
mercy
merely
mess
microphone
mighty
migrate
military
miner
mineral
mining
minister
miracle
miser
miserable
mission
missionary
Mister
modest
molasses
mold
mole
monk
monster
mosquito

moth
motto
muffle
multiplication
multiply
mumps
muscle
mush
musical

N
nag
napkin
native
neglect
Negro
nerve
nickname
niece
nimble
noble
nostril
notch
notion
nudge
nugget
numb
nursery

O
obedient
oblige
observe
obtain
occasion
octopus
odd
official
old-fashioned
olive
operate
operator
opportunity
oppose
original
orphan
otherwise
outfit
outwit
oxen
oxygen
oyster

P
pace
pajamas
pal
panic
pansy
panther

pantry
papoose
parakeet
parallel
pardon
parka
parlor
passage
patience
patio
patrol
peak
peasant
pebble
peck
peculiar
peer
pep
perch
perfume
peril
perish
permit
perplex
petroleum
petticoat
philosopher
phonograph
physical
picket
pickle
pier
pierce
pill
pineapple
pistol
plank
plantation
plaster
plead
pleasure
pledge
plod
plot
pluck
plume
plump
P.M.
pod
poem
poisonous
polo
poncho
population
porcupine
pore
postage
poster
pouch

pounce
poverty
practical
preach
presence
pressure
prevent
prey
principal
principle
proceed
produce
product
profit
progress
project
prompt
pronunciation
prop
propeller
proper
properly
provide
prowl
public
pudding
pulley
punch
purchase
pure
purse

Q
quail
quality
quarantine

R
raid
rail
rally
ram
ransom
rascal
raven
ravine
raw
ray
reasonable
recently
recess
reckon
reed
reel
reflect
reflection
refreshment
refuge
refugee

regard
regiment
region
regret
rehearse
rejoice
relative
relax
release
rely
remark
remarkable
repay
reputation
resolution
restaurant
review
revolution
revolutionary
rhyme
rhythm
ridiculous
rink
rinse
rip
ripple
risk
rod
roller
rotten
rove
rudder
rugged
rung
rust

S
sacrifice
saint
salary
salmon
sample
sandal
sap
sapling
satellite
scalp
scant
scar
scarlet
scheme
scholar
schooner
science
scorn
scrap
scrape
screw
scrub
scuffle

—————————— **EDL Reading Core Vocabulary—Graded Lists** ——————————

scurry
secretary
section
secure
seek
seep
seethe
seldom
select
semester
separate
sergeant
series
serpent
settlement
severe
shack
shaft
shaggy
shear
shield
shimmer
shock
shrill
shrink
shrub
shudder
shuffle
sickness
sin
sincere
sincerely
sinew
sip
situation
sketch
slab
slash
slave
slice
slick
slight
sly
smother
snare
snatch
sneer
snug
sob
sober
social
society
sod
soda
sofa
soil
sole
solemn
solid
sombrero

soothe
sorrow
sought
soul
souvenir
spade
spaghetti
sparrow
sped
spice
spinach
spite
splendid
sprain
sprawl
spun
spur
sputter
squash
squint
squire
squirm
stain
stationary
stationery
steak
stew
stitch
stock
stoop
strait
strife
stroll
strut
stub
stubborn
student
stun
stunt
sturdy
style
subject
subtract
subtraction
successful
suck
suggestion
sulphur
sunk
superintendent
survey
suspicious
sway
sweat
swirl
symbol
synonym
syrup
system

T tablet
tack
talent
task
tassel
tatter
tawny
tax
taxi
telegram
telegraph
temple
tend
tennis.
term
terrace
terrific
terrify
territory
textile
thatch
thaw
theater
theory
thermostat
thicket
thimble
thrash
thrilling
thrive
throb
thrown
thrust
thud
thus
tickle
timber
timid
tinder
tinker
tinsel
title
tobacco
toboggan
toil
topic
torch
torn
tortillas
total
tour
tourist
tournament
tow
trace
traitor
transport
transportation
tremendous

trench
trestle
trial
trickle
trifle
triumph
troop
trough
troupe
tulip
tundra
twig
twilight
twirl

U underneath
undertake
universe
university
upward

V vaccination
vacuum
vague
vain
valuable
value
vanity
various
vast
vehicle
veil
verse
vessel
vice president
vicious
victim
vinegar
violet
violin
visible
vision
volley
volunteer
vote

W wade
warehouse
wares
warmth
wax
wealth
weapon
wedding
wedge
whisk
whoop

widow
width
windshield
wit
wither
witness
worship
woven
wreath
wrestle

Y yarn
yelp
yoke
yonder
youth

EDL Reading Core Vocabulary—Graded Lists

Reading—6

A
absence
absolutely
absurd
abundant
abuse
accidentally
accomplish
accomplishment
accordion
accurate
accustomed
acid
acquaint
acquaintance
acquire
active
activity
actress
additional
adjustment
adore
adult
advertise
advertisement
advertising
affair
affection
aft
agreeable
agreement
ailing
aircraft
alas
album
alert
alfalfa
alien
allegiance
allowance
ally
alphabetical
altar
alternate
amateur
amazement
ambition
ambulance
amen
annoy
annual
antique
anxiety
apparently
applaud
applause
apply

appoint
appointment
appropriate
approval
approve
aqualung
archaeologist
architect
architecture
arena
argument
armistice
arouse
arrival
artificial
ascend
ascent
ashore
asphalt
assemble
assign
assignment
assist
assistance
assistant
association
assume
assure
astronomer
athlete
atom
atomic
attain
attendant
attire
attitude
attractive
auction
author
authority
available
avalanche
avenge
aviation
aviator
awe
axis
axle

B
backward
bade
badger
bald
ballot
banquet
barb
barber
barely
barge

baron
barren
bass
baton
bazaar
beacon
beckon
beech
beggar
behalf
behold
belief
belly
beloved
betray
beware
billion
biscuit
bishop
blacksmith
bleed
blot
blouse
boiler
bond
boom
boost
boundary
bounty
breast
brief
brier
brim
broadcast
broil
brood
brow
bulk
bulldozer
bulletin
bumper
bureau
bust
butler

C
cadet
calico
campaign
candidate
canopy
capable
capacity
carbon
career
caribou
carton
cartoon
cash
casket

catalog
caterpillar
cathedral
catsup
caution
cease
celery
cemetery
chap
characteristic
charity
chat
chemist
childhood
chirp
chord
chute
cider
cigar
cigarette
circular
citizenship
civilization
clad
clamber
clamp
clasp
click
cockpit
combat
combination
combine
comic
commence
commercial
commission
communicate
communication
comparison
complaint
compose
compound
conceal
conclude
conclusion
condemn
conduct
conference
confine
conflict
confusion
connection
conquest
conscience
conservation
considerable
consideration
consist
constant
constitution

contact
contents
continual
contract
contraption
contrary
contribute
core
corps
correspond
correspondent
corridor
costly
couch
cougar
counsel
coupon
courageous
courteous
courtesy
cramp
crate
create
criminal
crisis
crisscross
critical
criticize
cruise
crumple
crunch
crutch
cube
cubic
cuddle
cuff
cultivate
cunning
curse
curtsy
cushion
customary
cycle
cyclone
cylinder
cypress

D
dagger
dandelion
daze
debate
decay
deceive
decent
decimal
decline
decoration
dedicate
defense

EDL Reading Core Vocabulary—Graded Lists

definite
definition
defy
delegate
democracy
democratic
demon
departure
deposit
depth
derrick
description
despair
destination
destruction
determination
detour
devil
devote
devotion
devour
diagonal
diagram
diameter
diary
dice
diet
differ
dignified
discourage
discussion
disdain
disk
dislike
dismal
display
disposition
dispute
dissolve
distinct
distinguish
distinguished
distract
distribute
distrust
disturbance
document
dome
doom
dose
doze
draft
drape
drench
drug
druggist
duchess
duel
duet
dummy

dungeon
durable
dwelling

E economics
edition
eel
elaborate
elastic
elder
element
elementary
elevation
elk
embankment
ember
emblem
emerge
empire
employ
employee
employer
employment
enable
enchant
endure
energy
engage
enrage
enthusiasm
entry
erect
erosion
error
escort
essay
essential
estate
estimate
etc.
evaporate
eventual
evident
exact
exceedingly
execute
exert
exist
existence
exit
expand
expense
exploration
explosive
expose
extent
extreme
extremely

F fable
fake
false
fang
fascinate
fatal
fate
fatigue
feat
feature
federal
feeble
fender
fetch
film
fir
flax
flea
fled
fleece
flit
flourish
fluid
flush
foe
folly
forbid
ford
forecast
foreman
forfeit
forlorn
formal
formation
former
fortress
foul
foundation
founder
fowl
fragrant
frail
frequent
fret
friction
fringe
frisky
fro
fudge
fulfill
fumble
funnel
furthermore
fuse

G gag
gaily
gallant
gallery
galley
gangplank
garter
gem
genius
gently
genuine
geranium
gesture
gigantic
glossy
gnat
goggles
gorgeous
gossip
govern
gracious
graduate
graduation
grief
grieve
grizzly
groom
grope
grove
grub
guilty
gulf
gully
gutter
guy

H handicap
handy
hangar
hanger
harmonica
harsh
hasten
hatchet
hazel
headquarters
hedge
heed
helm
hem
herald
heroine
herring
hesitation
hibernate
hideous
hinder
hint
historical

hobble
hoist
homely
honorable
hood
hornet
horrid
host
hostess
household
hue
hydrogen
hyphen

I icicle
ideal
identify
idiot
idol
ignorance
ignorant
illustration
image
imitation
immigrant
imp
impolite
importance
impose
impress
impression
impulse
incident
income
indent
independent
indicate
individual
industry
infant
influence
inform
inherit
initial
injure
injury
insane
insert
inspection
inspire
install
instinct
institute
insult
intense
interfere
interior
international
interview
introduction

EDL Reading Core Vocabulary—Graded Lists

invade
invalid
investigate
involve
inward
issue
italics
item
ivy

J jagged
jay
jeans
jest
joint
jolt
judgment
jury

K keel
keg
kennel
kerchief
kindle

L label
lace
ladle
lag
lance
lanky
lard
lark
lash
lasso
latch
lather
latitude
laundry
laurel
layer
leadership
lecture
legal
legion
leisure
lens
lest
levy
liar
lichen
lilac
literature
litter
liver
livestock
local

location
loop
loosen
lope
luggage
lull
lurk
luxury

M macaroni
magnificent
maintain
majestic
major
majority
manager
manicure
mankind
mansion
mantle
manual
manure
manuscript
marine
marriage
marshmallow
mathematics
mature
measles
mechanic
mechanical
meddle
medical
medium
mellow
melon
memorize
menace
mental
mermaid
meteor
meter
method
mid
midst
mild
miniature
mink
minor
mint
mischievous
misfortune
missile
mite
mitt
mob
mock
moist
moisture
monitor

monstrous
monument
mooring
moral
mortal
mourn
movement
mow
muskrat
mustard
mutton
muzzle

N naked
narrator
naval
navigation
navigator
necessity
needy
nestle
nick
nigh
nightmare
nitrogen
normal
notify
nozzle
numeral
numerous
nylon

O oath
objection
observation
obvious
occasional
occupation
occupy
occur
odor
offend
offense
ooze
opera
operation
opposition
oral
orchestra
ore
organize
origin
orphanage
ostrich
ounce
outline
outrage
outrigger
outstanding

oval
overboard
overlook
overtake

P pageant
painful
pane
panel
paradise
parcel
parliament
pastime
patriot
patriotic
patriotism
pave
pavement
peacock
peal
pecan
peddle
peg
pelt
per
percent
performance
permanent
personal
personality
perspiration
pest
petrify
pew
phantom
pheasant
photograph
photographer
phrase
physician
pint
plastic
plateau
platter
plea
plentiful
pliers
plumber
plunder
plural
plus
poet
poetry
political
politics
ponder
porcelain
pork
porridge
portable

portion
positive
possess
posture
poultry
powerful
prefer
presidential
presume
prevail
prevention
previous
priest
primary
prime
privilege
process
procession
proclaim
production
profession
professional
profitable
promote
promotion
proportion
propose
prospect
prow
prune
publish
publisher
pulp
pulse
punishment
purify

Q quaint
qualify
quantity
quarry
quiz
quotation

R rabbi
radar
radiator
radish
raft
railway
raisin
ramp
rampart
rank
rap
rapid
raspberry
rate
ration

23

EDL Reading Core Vocabulary—Graded Lists

readily
reap
reassure
rebel
receipt
recent
recipe
recite
reckless
recommend
recover
recreation
reduce
reef
refer
referee
reference
refine
reform
refusal
regardless
register
regulation
relate
relation
relationship
relay
relieve
religion
religious
remedy
remote
replace
representative
reptile
republic
request
require
research
resemble
resent
reserve
reservoir
resign
resist
resistance
resolve
resort
respectful
respond
response
responsibility
restore
retire
retort
revenge
reverse
revive
revolve
revolver

rig
rigid
rival
rogue
romantic
rot
rotary
rouse
rubbish
ruffle
rummage
rumor
rural
rut
rye

S sacred
sag
sash
satin
satisfaction
saucer
scan
schedule
scientific
scribble
script
scroll
seam
secondary
selection
senate
senator
senior
sensation
sensible
sentry
sermon
session
shabby
shame
shampoo
shatter
shave
sheer
shellac
shilling
shingle
shred
shrimp
shutter
signature
similar
site
skeleton
skid
skillful
skull
slack
slain

slang
slate
slaughter
slavery
slay
sledge
sleek
sleet
slim
sling
slit
slot
slumber
slump
slung
slush
smash
smear
smuggle
snack
snail
snicker
snore
snout
soccer
socket
solar
solo
solution
soot
source
sow
span
spangle
spaniel
species
specimen
spiral
spit
splinter
sponge
spout
sprinkle
sprint
sprout
spruce
sprung
spurt
squadron
squirt
stab
staff
stag
stale
stammer
standard
starboard
starch
steward
stingy
storage

stork
stow
strand
strawberry
strict
strode
structure
strung
stubble
studio
stung
submarine
submerge
submit
substance
substitute
sufficient
suitable
summit
summon
superior
superstition
supreme
surf
suspend
suspense
suspension
swap
swat
swear
swollen
swore
sworn
sympathetic
sympathy

T tackle
tangerine
taper
tarpaulin
tavern
technical
tempt
tense
tentacle
text
thee
theft
theme
thermometer
thirst
thistle
thong
thorough
thou
threat
throttle
throughout
thy
tidy
tingle

tint
tissue
token
toll
tomb
tone
torment
tornado
torpedo
torture
trample
translate
transparent
trapeze
trash
tread
treason
treatment
trek
trespass
triangle
tribute
trigger
triumphant
trolley
tropics
truant
tuna
tunic
turban
turf
tusk
tutor
twine
twitch
typical
tyrant

U unexpected
union
unravel
urgent
utensil

V vacant
vagabond
valve
van
vanilla
vapor
variety
varnish
vault
vegetation
vein
venture
vertical
vest
vibrate

vibration
vice
vicinity
vigor
virus
vivid
volume
vow
vowel
vulture

W waffle
wages
waiter
wallet
walnut
waltz
ward
wardrobe
warily
wart
wasp
wealthy
weird
wept
westward
wheeze
whimper
wondrous
wrath
wren
wrench
wring

X X-ray

Y yacht
yam
yeast
yield
yolk
youngster

Z zigzag

EDL Reading Core Vocabulary—Graded Lists

Reading—7

A
abdomen
abroad
abrupt
absolute
accuracy
ace
acknowledge
acknowledgment
actual
acute
adhesive
adjoining
administration
admittance
advancement
aerial
aeronautics
affectionate
afloat
aged
agile
agony
ajar
algebra
alias
alibi
alliance
alloy
almanac
alteration
alto
ambitious
ambush
amend
amendment
ammonia
amusement
anguish
anniversary
annoyance
antler
apology
apparatus
appendicitis
appendix
approximate
approximately
apt
arc
archery
armory
arsenal
artillery
asbestos
assassinate
assault

assembly
associate
assortment
assurance
astronomy
asylum
atlas
attraction
await
awning

B
bachelor
baffle
bail
balk
ballad
ballet
balm
ban
banish
baptize
barbecue
barometer
barrier
bashful
basic
basis
bask
batch
beau
becalm
begrudge
belfry
belittle
beseech
biography
blackmail
bleak
blindfold
bliss
blockade
blunt
bombard
bonus
boomerang
boulevard
bracket
brew
bribe
bristle
brittle
broth
brutal
brute
buffet
bungalow
bunt
burial
burlap

burr
buzzard

C
caddie
calculate
campus
cancel
cancer
cannibal
cantaloupe
canteen
carcass
carload
carnation
cartridge
cashier
cavern
cavity
chairman
changeable
chapel
chariot
chasm
chauffeur
chef
cherish
chess
chivalry
cinnamon
circulate
circumference
circumstances
civic
civics
clan
clause
climax
clot
coffin
cog
collapse
colossal
comedy
comet
commerce
commit
commotion
compartment
compel
compete
competition
complexion
complicate
compromise
conceit
conceive
confront
considerate
consume
consumer

contagious
continuous
contrast
convey
conveyor
conviction
coop
cooperative
cordial
corpse
correspondence
coupé
cram
crease
creative
creed
crevice
crimson
critic
criticism
croquet
crusade
cue
cultural
culture
curio

D
dealer
dealt
debtor
decoy
defiance
define
defrost
demerit
Democrat
depart
dependent
deputy
derby
descent
desirable
desolate
despisc
despite
destiny
detect
development
devise
dialogue
diaper
digest
digestion
dimple
director
directory
disable
disagree
disagreeable
disarm

discard
discount
dishonest
disinfectant
disobey
disorder
disown
displease
distinction
divine
domestic
donate
donation
donor
dormitory
doubtful
drama
dramatic
drapery
dual
dwell

E
ebony
effective
efficient
elevate
elope
embarrassment
emphasize
enforce
engrave
enlarge
enlist
enroll
enthusiastic
entitle
environment
era
erupt
eternal
eternity
exaggerate
exceed
exception
excursion
executive
exhale
exile
expectant
expel
exposure

F
fabric
factor
fad
falsehood
falter
famine
fantastic

25

fathom
favorable
fearless
fee
feminine
ferocious
feud
fickle
fiction
fiend
filter
filth
flask
flatter
flaw
flimsy
flirt
florist
focus
foil
folder
foliage
formerly
formula
fracture
fragile
fragment
frank
frankfurter
freak
freshman
frigid
fumes
fund
fundamental

G
gallows
gamble
gangster
gargle
gauge
gaunt
generator
geological
geologist
geology
geyser
gland
glint
gloat
gong
gorilla
graph
groove
gross
grudge
guarantee
guardian

H hardy
harmony
haste
hatred
hearse
heave
heifer
heir
heiress
hemisphere
hermit
hiccup
hobo
holdup
horizontal
hostile
hub
humane
humanity
humid
humidity
hydrant
hypnotize

I illustrate
imprison
improvise
incomplete
incredible
indigestion
industrious
infect
inferior
infinite
influential
influenza
informal
ingredient
initiate
initiation
injection
inscription
institution
instructor
insurance
insure
intellectual
intensive
intention
intermediate
investigation
irregular
isle
isolate

J jazz
jeer
jetty
jilt
jubilant

K khaki
kidnap
kiln
kin
kink
knapsack
knead
knuckle

L laborer
lacquer
laden
landscape
lapel
latter
lavender
legible
levee
liable
lieutenant
limber
linger
linoleum
liquor
lisp
lobby
lobster
longitude
loot
lubricate
lullaby
lure
lye

M mahogany
mallet
mammal
mangle
maniac
margin
marshal
masculine
massive
matinee
melancholy
menu
merchandise
mercury
mere
merit
mesh

meteorite
microscope
microscopic
midget
mileage
millionaire
mimic
mingle
minnow
minority
miraculous
mirage
mirth
misery
mistletoe
misty
misunderstand
mobile
moderate
modify
monarch
monopoly
monotonous
mosaic
municipal
mural
murder
muscular
mutiny

N narrative
nasal
nausea
neon
neutral
nipple
noose
notable
novel
novelty
nude
nun

O objective
obligation
obstacle
omen
opponent
option
orchid
organization
ornamental
outlet
overcome
overdue
oversight
ownership

P pamphlet
paralyze
parch
parchment
pare
parole
partial
participate
particle
passion
pastor
pastry
patent
payment
pendulum
penetrate
peninsula
penitentiary
pension
periscope
perishable
perpetual
persecute
persist
petal
phase
phenomenon
philanthropist
picturesque
pitiful
plague
plaque
platinum
plywood
poise
policy
poll
pose
postpone
pout
prank
precede
precision
predict
preferable
preference
prejudice
premium
preside
prestige
primitive
probable
progressive
prohibit
prominent
prong
propel
proposal
proposition
proprietor

EDL Reading Core Vocabulary—Graded Lists

prospector
province
provision
pry
psalm
publication
publicity
punctual
punctuate
punctuation
puncture
pursue
pursuit
putty
pyramid

Q
qualification
quartet
quench
quest

R
radiant
radius
rafter
rash
rave
rayon
razor
realm
rebellion
rebuild
recall
reception
recital
recitation
recognition
recollection
rectangle
reek
refund
regain
regulator
reign
reject
relent
reliable
reluctant
remainder
remembrance
remnant
render
renew
rental
representation
Republican
reside
residence
resident
residential

respiration
restless
reveal
riot
rivalry
rivet
roach
robot
rodent
role
romance
roommate
roost
rotate
rotation
routine

S
saliva
salvage
sane
sanitarium
sanitary
sardine
satchel
satisfactory
scald
scaly
scenic
scoff
scour
sculptor
sculpture
scum
secrecy
sedan
sentiment
sentimental
serial
serum
sewer
sex
sheath
shrewd
shrine
shrivel
shroud
siege
sift
sire
slime
slogan
slum
smoulder
smudge
snob
solitary
sovereign
spectacular
spectator
speculate

speedometer
sphere
spire
splint
sportsmanship
spry
squad
stadium
staple
starvation
statesman
steeple
stenographer
sterilize
stifle
strangle
stucco
subdue
subscribe
subscription
suburb
succession
sue
suicide
suite
suitor
sulk
sullen
supervise
supervisor
surge
survive
suspenders
suspicion
sustain
swoon
symphony
symptom
synagogue

T
tallow
talon
tapestry
tariff
tattoo
tedious
tempest
temptation
tenor
terminal
testify
testimony
tether
thigh
thresh
tongs
tonic
torrent
tract
tradition

tragic
trait
transom
treacherous
trio
triple
trophy
trowel
truce
tuberculosis
turbulent
turnpike
turpentine
turret
typhoon

U
unique
unruly
upheld
uranium
urn
utilize
utmost
utter

V
valiant
vary
vat
vaudeville
venison
venom
vent
version
veteran
via
victorious
vigorous
vile
villain
violence
violent
vise
vital
vitamin
vocabulary
vomit
vulcanize
vulgar

W
warden
warp
warrant
wary
waver
wed
weld

welfare
welt
whim
wilt
wretched

EDL Reading Core Vocabulary—Graded Lists

Reading—8

A
abbreviate
abbreviation
abnormal
abode
abolish
academic
accelerate
acceptance
access
accessible
accessory
acclaim
accommodate
accommodation
accumulate
acquit
acreage
actuate
adequate
adjacent
adjourn
admirable
adolescent
adorn
adrift
advisable
adviser
advocate
affirm
affirmative
aggravate
aghast
aide
ailment
alcoholic
allay
aloof
ambassador
amiable
amid
amphibious
ample
analyze
anatomy
anesthesia
anesthetic
annex
anthem
anticipate
antidote
antiseptic
apparel
appease
appliance
applicant

application
ardent
aristocrat
armament
array
arson
artery
aspect
assert
atone
attachment
attentive
attorney
authentic
authorize
auxiliary

B
ballast
bandanna
bankrupt
barbarian
barnacle
barricade
battalion
beneficial
besiege
beverage
bias
bide
binoculars
blare
blemish
blight
bloated
blotter
boarder
bondage
boon
boredom
borne
bout
bravery
brawl
brawn
breach
breadth
bred
brigade
brink
broker
browse
brunt
budget
buoyancy

C
cache
calamity
calorie

camouflage
capsize
carburetor
careen
caress
cascade
casserole
casualty
catapult
cavalry
censor
census
certify
chaplain
char
charter
chassis
chime
choral
chowder
chromium
circuit
cistern
civilian
clamor
clarify
classic
classification
classify
cleanse
clearance
clergy
client
clinic
clog
clutter
coincidence
collide
collision
columnist
coma
comedian
communism
competent
comprehend
computer
conditional
confederate
confer
confetti
confidential
confirm
conform
consequence
consequently
consistent
consolation
console
conspicuous
conspiracy
constable

consul
contaminate
contempt
contradict
controversy
convert
convict
convoy
cope
copyright
corporal
corporation
corrode
corrupt
counterfeit
courtship
coy
cruelty
culprit
cumbersome
curdle
curfew
currency
curry
custody
cutlery

D
debris
decade
deceit
deception
decipher
decompose
deduct
defect
defective
defendant
deflate
deflect
deformity
delicatessen
delirious
deluge
demolish
denial
denim
dental
deport
depress
depression
deprive
derive
detain
detest
devout
dictate
dictator
dilute
dimension

diminish
din
dingy
diploma
diplomat
dirigible
discharge
discipline
discriminate
dishonor
disinherit
dislocate
dislodge
dispatch
dispense
displace
disprove
disregard
disrespect
dissatisfied
distort
distribution
dividend
divorce
doctrine
dominate
doubtless
douse
drab
drastic
drawl
dredge
drunkard
duplicate
duration

E
earshot
eaves
eclipse
economical
economy
edible
edit
editorial
efficiency
eject
elapse
elated
electrocute
eligible
eliminate
elude
emancipation
embargo
embassy
embrace
emerald
emigrant
emigrate

EDL Reading Core Vocabulary—Graded Lists

emotion
emphasis
enact
encircle
enclosure
encompass
encounter
endanger
endeavor
endorse
endow
energetic
enfold
enrich
enrollment
entangle
envelop
envious
epidemic
episode
equality
escalator
etiquette
evacuate
evade
evasive
excel
excess
exclamation
exclude
exclusive
exempt
expectation
exposition
exquisite
extension
exterior
external
extinct
extinguish
extract
extraordinary

F
facial
facilities
facility
faculty
fanatic
fantasy
faulty
fiancé
fiancée
fidget
finance
financial
fixture
flannel
flexible
flinch
floral

flounder
flue
fluorescent
fluster
fondle
fore
foremost
forestry
foretell
forgery
fortify
fortitude
fossil
foyer
fraud
frenzy
frill
frolic
fugitive
function
furlough
fuselage

G
gadget
gait
galvanized
garlic
gaudy
genial
geometry
gill
gilt
girder
gospel
graft
grotto
guttural

H
habitation
haggard
haphazard
haughty
haven
hazard
hectic
hence
hereditary
heredity
heroic
hilarious
hilt
hinderance
hoard
homicide
honorary
horde
horsepower
hospitable

hostage
hurtle

I
identical
identification
identity
ignite
illegal
illuminate
immerse
immigration
immortal
immortality
immune
impact
impair
impart
imperfect
implement
implore
impressive
imprint
improper
impurity
inability
inaugurate
incapable
incense
incentive
incompetent
inconvenience
indefinite
indifferent
indulge
infantile
inflammable
inflate
inflict
infuriate
inhale
inlaid
inmate
inoculate
inquiry
insolent
inspiration
installation
installment
instill
insulation
integrate
intercept
intermission
internal
intersection
intimate
intoxicate
intricate
intrigue

intrude
invasion
inventory
invert
invest
investment
irk
irritate

J
jaunt
jovial
juror
justify
juvenile

L
lapse
lavatory
laxative
leaflet
lease
lecturer
ledger
lessen
liberal
liberate
lilt
literary
livelihood
livid
loathe
locality
logic
logical
lotion
lottery
lounge
lubricant
lunatic
lynch
lyrics

M
macadam
maestro
maim
maintenance
makeshift
maneuver
maroon
martyr
mason
masquerade
massacre
massage
masterpiece
matrimony
matron
maximum

maze
meager
memorandum
merge
midday
milestone
militia
minimum
miscellaneous
mishap
misjudge
mislead
misplace
mobilize
mode
molar
molecular
molecule
molest
molten
monarchy
monastery
morale
morality
morgue
morsel
mortar
mortgage
motive
multiple
multitude
munitions
musty
mutilate
mystify
mythology

N
naturalize
negative
nomad
nominate
nomination
nominee
noticeable
notorious
nourish
nymph

O
oblong
observatory
obstruct
occupant
occurrence
offensive
ointment
omit
omitted
oppress

EDL Reading Core Vocabulary—Graded Lists

oppression
optical
orator
ordeal
outcast
outgrowth
outskirts
overcast
overhaul
overlap
overlay

P
pacify
pact
pagan
pamper
pantomime
paralysis
parish
partition
passport
pastel
pasteurize
pathetic
pauper
pawn
pedestal
pedestrian
pedigree
penalize
penalty
penthouse
perfection
perforate
perimeter
periodical
perpendicular
persistence
pertain
perturb
petition
petty
pharmacy
photostat
physicist
physics
piety
pious
piston
pitfall
pivot
placard
plaid
plasma
plight
plumage
ply
pneumonia
poach

politician
pollen
pollute
portfolio
portrait
portray
possibility
posterity
postscript
potential
potion
precipice
precipitation
precise
predicament
prefabricated
prepaid
prescribe
prescription
pretense
preview
prim
prior
privacy
probability
probe
procedure
proclamation
profile
profound
projector
prolong
prone
propaganda
prophecy
prophet
propulsion
prosecute
prosper
prosperity
prosperous
protrude
proverb
provisional
provoke
pulpit
purity
pygmy

Q
quake
questionnaire
quizzical
quota
quote

R
racial
radium
rant
rarity

ratio
reaction
readiness
reality
recede
receptacle
recline
recoil
recommendation
recorder
recovery
recruit
recur
reduction
reflex
refrain
refresh
registration
regrettable
rehearsal
reinforce
relapse
reliance
relic
relish
remit
remorse
removal
renegade
renewal
renounce
repeal
repel
repent
repertory
repetition
reprieve
reproduce
reproduction
requirement
requisition
resource
resourceful
respectable
restrain
restraint
restrict
resume
retail
retain
revelation
revenue
reverence
reverend
revise
revision
rheumatism
rout
rustic
ruthless

S
Sabbath
saga
salve
sanctuary
sanitation
scaffold
scandal
scorch
scoundrel
scripture
sect
security
sensitive
sentinel
sequence
serenade
shirk
shortage
shun
sieve
signify
singe
singular
sinister
siphon
skyscraper
slander
sophomore
soprano
sparse
specific
specification
specify
spiritual
splice
sponsor
stamina
stanza
static
steadfast
stench
sterling
stratosphere
strenuous
strive
subordinate
substantial
subtle
suffocate
sultry
summary
superb
surgeon
surgery
surplus
survival
survivor
swerve
swindle

swivel
synopsis
systematic

T
taboo
tact
tarnish
taunt
temperate
temporary
tendency
tenement
testament
torrid
tragedy
trance
transform
transit
transmission
transmit
transplant
tremor
trend
trump
tuition

U
unanimous
unison
universal
upholster
uproar

V
vacancy
valet
valor
vandal
variation
varsity
velocity
veneer
vengeance
ventilate
veranda
verdict
verge
versus
veto
vineyard
violate
virgin
virtue
visor
vocal
vocation
void
vouch

W
wholly
wield
wily
writhe

Y
yearn

Z
zeal
zest

EDL Reading Core Vocabulary—Graded Lists

Reading—9

A

a la carte
abate
abhor
abolition
abominable
abound
absentee
abstract
abyss
accomplice
accord
accusation
adaptable
adaptation
adhere
administer
adversary
adverse
affliction
aggressive
agitate
alcove
allotment
amass
amplify
amputate
analysis
anecdote
antagonize
appraise
apprehend
aptitude
aquatic
arbitrary
arid
armory
aroma
arrogant
artesian
articulate
assent
asset
attribute
audible
audition
autobiography
avail
avert

B

banister
barracks
baste
bayonet
beige
belligerent
benediction
bestow
bewitch
bibliography
billiards
bleach
booty
bosom
brazen
buffer

C

caliber
canvass
caper
capitalize
caption
captivate
captivity
catastrophe
category
cauldron
celebrity
chafe
champagne
chide
cinema
circumstance
cleave
clerical
clique
coincide
combustion
commend
commodity
commute
comparable
compensation
complex
comply
compress
compulsory
compute
concede
concession
concise
confiscate
congestion
congregation
conscientious
consecutive
conservative
constellation
contemplate
contemporary
contestant
continuity
contour
contraction
conventional
converge
conversion
convertible
coordination
coronation
corrugated
cosmetics
countenance
counteract
cower
cram
crave
creation
crescent
crochet
cult
custodian

D

damnable
data
dauntless
dean
debatable
deceased
decisive
deem
deface
defensive
dejected
delete
deliberate
delinquent
denomination
denounce
density
deplore
desertion
destitute
detach
detention
detract
diction
diplomacy
dire
disapprove
disastrous
disband
disbelief
disciple
disclose
discomfort
disconnect
discontent
discontinue
discord
disembark
disengage
disfigure

E

earthy
ebb
ecstasy
embalm
embezzle
encore
endear
entice
entrust
enviable
envoy
equivalent
err
escapade
espionage
evolution
evolve
exalt
expanse
expansion
expend
expenditure
expire
exterminate
extravagant
extremity

F

famished
farce
fatality
feint
felony
ferment
festive
feudal
filament
fillet
filtration
flair
flank

dismantle
disorganized
dispossess
disqualify
disrupt
distasteful
diverge
diversion
divert
divulge
doff
domain
dowry
drudgery
duly
dutiful
dwindle

flaw
flicker
foreboding
foresight
forgo
formidable
foundry
fraternity
fray
fumigate

G

gaiety
galaxy
garrison
gild
gist
glamour
glorify
grievance
grimace
gruesome
guidance

H

harmonize
heathen
homage
hoodwink

I

idolize
illegible
illiterate
illusion
impersonate
imply
imposter
improbable
impudent
impulsive
inborn
incurable
indebted
indelible
indispensable
inertia
infantry
infirmary
inflation
ingenious
insight
insignia
insignificant
insomnia
instantaneous
intact
intangible
integrity
irresistible

———— EDL Reading Core Vocabulary—Graded Lists ————

irritable
isthmus
itemize

J judicial

L lament
landmark
lavish
legislature
legitimate
limousine
livery
loiter
lore
luminous
lust

M magistrate
malicious
mechanism
medieval
meditate
memorable
menagerie
misconduct
misguided
mistrust
momentary
monogram
mortify
mute
mutual

N nasal
nationality
nautical
navigable
noteworthy

O obscure
obsolete
obstinate
optimistic
ordain
originate
ornate
overpower
overwhelm

P parasite
pending
pennant
perceive
personal
pewter
physique
pilfer
platoon
porous
precaution
preface
prefix
prehistoric
priority
prism
probation
projection
propel

Q quadruple

R random
rapture
ravage
rebound
redeem
refinery
refrain
regal
regime
remedial
renown
replica
reprimand
reproach
reprove
repulsive
retard
retract
retrieve
righteous
robust
rove

S sanity
sarcasm
secrete
semicircle
serene
sever
sham
shank
siesta
sluggish
slur

smite
smock
smote
snub
specialist
spendthrift
spouse
spurn
squeamish
staunch
stealthy
strategy
stress
stricken
studious
sublime
subordinate
suffice
suffix
superficial
superfluous
supernatural
supplement
suppress
surly
surpass
swarthy

T tangible
tantrum
technique
telescope
tempo
tenant
tension
terminate
texture
thwart
titanic
tolerate
transaction
tripod
trivial
turmoil
twinge

U undertone
upheaval
urchin

V vacate
valise
vanquish
vendor
verify
vestibule

veterinary
vial

W wane
wayward
wean
wistful
withhold

EDL Reading Core Vocabulary—Graded Lists

Reading—10

A
accentuate
adept
affront
allay
allure
amphitheater
animation
annihilate
annul
anonymous
apex
appalling
appropriation
ardor
artisan
ashtray
assess
atrocious
auditory
aura
automation
axiom

B
bane
banter
bauble
bedlam
befall
belated
belie
benefactor
benevolent
bereaved
betroth
bevel
bevy
biology
bland
bogus
boisterous
bolster
brandish
buttress

C
callous
cancellation
canine
capillary
carat
carnivorous
cater
centennial
chagrin

chronic
clientele
colleague
collegiate
communicable
comparative
compile
complement
component
compulsion
concept
conclusive
confound
consolidate
consultant
contemptible
contraband
convalescent
conveyance
convulsion
coroner
cosmic
courier
credentials
creditor
crucial
crypt
cryptic
cull
cumulative
curriculum
curtail
curvature
cuticle
cynical

D
daily
debit
debutante
default
deficient
defile
deflation
deft
deity
delve
demented
demolition
demoralize
demure
dependent
depreciate
designate
despondent
deteriorate
devastate
dialect
diaphragm
dignitary

dilate
dilemma
diligent
dirge
disconcert
discretion
disillusion
disintegrate
dispel
dispensary
dispense
displacement
disreputable
dissect
disuse
diverse
dogged
dominant
dormant
dote
dregs
droll
duct
dupe
dynamic

E
eccentric
economize
elongate
eloquent
emancipate
embellish
emboss
embryo
emit
encampment
enhance
enlighten
enrapture
ensemble
enthrall
enumerate
enunciate
equilibrium
eradicate
esteem
ethical
evaluate
evasion
exasperate
exotic
exploit
exponent
expressly
exuberant

F
fallacy
feasible
feign
ferret
fictitious
finale
flail
flange
flaunt
focal
foible
folio
foreshorten
formulate
forum
fraught
frivolous
frontage
froth
frugal
frustrate
furtive
futile

G
gala
gaseous
gender
genteel
germinate
girth
glaze
glean
glib
glutton
gore
granulate
gratify
grotesque
grovel
guerrilla

H
hapless
havoc
heirloom
heritage
hew
hoax
horoscope
horticulture
hovel
humbug
humdrum
humiliate
humility
hybrid
hydraulic
hypocrite
hysteria

I
idiom
illegitimate
illogical
illustrious
immature
immeasurable
impartial
impeach
imperative
imperial
impersonal
impertinent
impoverish
impregnate
inaccessible
incandescent
incision
incite
inclination
inclusive
incorporate
incriminate
indisposed
induce
inducement
inert
inevitable
infatuate
infernal
infidel
inkling
inquisitive
insufferable
intensity
intolerable
intolerant
intuition
invertebrate
invigorating
invincible
invoke
ire
irony

J
jargon

L
laborious
lateral
legacy
liability
linear
liquidate
listless

EDL Reading Core Vocabulary—Graded Lists

M magnitude
mainstay
malady
manipulate
manor
marital
materialize
maternal
maternity
maul
mediocre
medley
mire
misconception
momentum
monologue
morbid
mutation
mystical

N naive
namesake
narcotic
narrate
necessitate
negotiate
nonchalant
notary
nucleus

O obituary
oblique
oblivion
obnoxious
obscene
opaque
oratory
ordinance
organic
organism
overture

P panorama
parochial
parry
passé
passive
paternal
patron
patronize
pensive
perception

perseverance
perspective
pertinent
pessimistic
petite
phenomenal
pictorial
pigment
pilgrimage
pinnacle
piteous
plausible
pliable
populate
portal
portly
precinct
predominant
pregnant
preliminary
prelude
premature
preoccupy
prestige
prevalent
profess
proficient
progression
prose
providence
provincial
prudent
psychiatrist
psychology
pulverize
putrid

Q qualm
quandary
quell

R radiate
radical
ratify
rational
ravenous
ravish
readjust
rebuff
reconcile
rectify
recuperate
reformatory
rehabilitate
reimburse
reinstate
remittance
rend

renovate
reorganize
reputable
residue
revel
reverie
revert
revoke
revue
rhapsody
rift
ritual
roster
rostrum
rue
rupture

S sally
satire
saturate
scavenger
scope
scrimmage
scrutinize
sear
secluded
sector
sediment
segment
segregate
silhouette
simultaneous
skeptical
skirmish
slothful
smelt
sodden
solitude
soluble
solvent
somber
sorority
spasm
spinster
spontaneous
stability
stagnant
stalwart
stance
sterile
stigma
stimulate
stolid
strata
strewn
stupefy
stupor
suave
subside

sundry
superimpose
superlative
superstructure
symmetry
synthetic

T tabulate
taint
tangent
tantalize
tart
tawdry
temperance
theorem
thermal
tier
timely
tolerable
torrid
torso
transcribe
transfusion
transpose
tributary
tumult

U ultimate
ultimatum
uncouth
unerring
unify
unkempt
urban
usage

V variable
vertebrate
vigil
vigilant
virtual
visualize
vitality

W waif
wan
wend
whet

EDL Reading Core Vocabulary—Graded Lists

Reading—11

A
abashed
abcess
abdicate
abrasion
abridge
abstain
accost
acquisition
acrid
adage
addict
adulterated
affable
affectation
affix
aftermath
aggression
algae
alienate
align
alimony
alleviate
alumni
ambiguous
amplitude
analogy
anesthetic
annals
antecedent
antiquated
aperture
arbitration
ascertain
ascribe
askew
asphyxiation
aspiration
assail
assimilate
atheist
attache
audit
aversion
awry

B
beneficiary
bequeath
biennial
bier
bilingual
binder
bizarre
botany
boudoir
boycott
brevity
broach
brusque
bulwark
burlesque
burnish

C
candid
capitalist
caricature
carouse
cataract
catechism
cavalcade
celestial
centrifugal
cessation
cite
claimant
collaborate
collective
commemorate
commentary
commune
compassion
compatible
complacent
composite
composure
concave
conception
concoct
concur
concussion
condescend
condiment
condolence
condone
conductive
confection
confederation
congeal
congenial
consecrate
constitute
contemptuous
contend
context
contortion
converse
convex
cosmopolitan
covet
criterion
cuisine
culinary
cyst

D
debonair
decrepit
defer
depict
deplete
derange
derelict
desirous
deter
detriment
deviate
devious
devoid
dexterity
diagnosis
differential
diffuse
dilapidated
discern
discourse
discredit
discrepancy
disdainful
disgorge
disheveled
disperse
disproportionate
dissimilar
dissociate
distraught
docile
doleful
drone
dubious
dynasty

E
eddy
egotism
elegy
elliptical
emaciated
eminent
emphatic
encumbered
engross
enliven
ensue
entail
epic
epitaph
equity
erratic
erroneous
essence
evoke
excerpt
excruciating
exhilarated
explicit
expulsion
extortion
exultation

F
fabricate
facet
facilitate
faction
fallow
fastidious
feline
fervent
fervor
fetter
fidelity
financier
fissure
flagrant
fluctuate
forage
forbearance
franchise
fraudulent

G
gauntlet
generalize
gibe
glower
glut
graphic
guise
gullible
gusto

H
habitable
habitat
hallucination
hulk
hypothesis

I
idealism
idolatry
imagery
immaculate
immaterial
immobile
impale
impassive
impediment
impending
imperil
implicate
impromptu
inadvertently
inane
inanimate
inaugurate
incapacitate
incendiary
incongruous
incredulous
increment
incur
indict
indignity
inept
infallible
infamous
infer
infest
infidelity
inflection
influx
informant
infringe
infuse
inherent
inhibition
initiative
innovation
inquest
inquisition
insensible
inseparable
insinuate
instigate
instrumental
insurrection
integral
interaction
intercede
interject
interloper
interlude
intermittent
intern
interrogate
intersperse
intervene
intimidate
intonation
intrusion
invaluable
invariably
inverse
invocation
invoice
irrelevant
irrepressible

J
jaded
jeopardize
jocular

_____ **EDL Reading Core Vocabulary—Graded Lists** _____

judicious
jurisdiction

K kindred
kinetic
knoll

L labyrinth
laxity
legation
lenient
lethal
lewd
liaison
libel
limpid
lineage
linguistic
literal
lobbyist
lunar
lustrous
luxuriant

M maladjustment
malice
malign
malignant
malleable
mandatory
mania
manifest
manifold
mannerism
marauder
materialistic
mausoleum
meander
memento
memoir
menial
mentor
metropolis
mettle
mien
misdemeanor
momentous
monetary
monotone
morose
motif
muse
myriad

N natal
nationalism
negligible
neurotic
neuter
nocturnal
nominal
noncommittal
nonexistent
notation
nullify
nutrient
nutritious

O obliterate
obsession
occult
odious
ominous
onslaught
opportune
orgy
orient
orientation
oscillate
overbearing

P pacifist
palatable
pallor
palpitate
parable
paradox
parley
partisan
pathos
patronage
peerless
penal
perennial
perjury
permeate
perpetrate
personnel
peruse
philanthropy
philosophy
physiology
pillage
placid
pollinate
polygamy
pompous
populace
populous
posterior
potent

precarious
premonition
preponderance
preposterous
presumptuous
primeval
procure
prodigal
profane
profuse
prohibition
projectile
promenade
propriety
prospectus
prostrate
proxy
psychosis
pugilist
pugnacious
purge

Q quadrant
query
quibble

R rabble
rabid
ramification
rampant
ransack
raucous
realist
rebate
recession
reciprocate
reclaim
reconnaissance
recourse
recurrence
redundant
refute
regent
regimen
rejuvenate
relinquish
reminiscent
remuneration
renaissance
renegade
replenish
repose
repress
reprisal
reproof
requisite
resolute
resonance

respective
resplendent
restoration
resurrection
retaliate
retention
retina
retribution
revulsion
ricochet
rigorous
rite
rote
ruse

S sanction
saunter
savory
scapegoat
scourge
scruple
secede
sedate
sedative
semblance
sensory
sensual
sequel
servitude
severance
simile
simulate
slovenly
sobriety
socialist
solace
solicit
spectrum
squander
stark
statistics
status
stereotype
stilt
stimulus
stint
stipulate
subsequent
subsistence
successor
suede
supple
surmise
surmount
susceptible
swathe
synchronize
syndicate
synthesis

T taut
tentative
tenure
tepid
terse
therapeutic
thesis
tincture
tirade
traction
tranquil
transgress
transition
translucent
transpire
traverse
treatise
trite
truism
tryst
typify

U ulterior
unfounded

V vagrant
valid
vanguard
vantage
variance
veer
vehement
versatile
vibrant
vie
vintage
virile
virtuoso
vivacious
vogue
vouch
voucher

W waiver
wanton
whimsical
wrangle

Z zenith
zodiac

EDL Reading Core Vocabulary—Graded Lists

Reading—12

A
abduct
aberration
abet
abeyance
abject
absolve
abstinence
abstraction
acclimate
accrue
acrimonious
acumen
adamant
adherent
admonish
adroit
advent
aesthetic
affidavit
affiliate
affinity
affluent
aggregate
agnostic
agrarian
allege
allegory
allocate
allude
altruistic
amalgamate
amenable
amenity
amicable
amity
amorphous
anarchy
anathema
animosity
annuity
apathy
apparition
arable
archives
arduous
askance
aspersion
astringent
astute
atrophy
audacity
augment
austerity
autocracy
avid
avocation

B
baleful
banal
beguile
bigot
blasphemy
bourgeois
bureaucracy

C
cadaverous
candor
cantankerous
capitulate
carnage
caste
caucus
caustic
cede
censure
cerebral
characterize
charlatan
chaste
chasten
chastise
chattel
circumvent
citation
coerce
cogitate
coherent
cohort
collateral
colloquial
comely
communal
complicity
comprise
concentric
conciliate
conclave
concourse
confidant
conjecture
connive
connoisseur
conscription
consensus
constituent
constraint
contrive
convene
conversant
corollary
correlate
crass
credible
credulous
culminate

D
debase
decadence
decry
deference
definitive
defray
defunct
degenerate
deify
delineation
delude
delusion
demagogue
demeanor
denote
depraved
deride
derivative
desist
despicable
despot
desultory
detonate
differentiate
diffident
digression
diminutive
disconsolate
discreet
disparage
disseminate
dissent
dissertation
dissipate
dissonant
dissuade
distend
dogmatic
domicile
dub
duplicity
duress

E
ecclesiastical
echelon
edict
ediface
effervescence
effigy
effrontery
electorate
elixir
emanate
embody
embroiled
ensconced
entreat
epoch

F
facetious
facsimile
felicity
festoon
fetid
fiasco
figment
figuratively
finesse
firmament
fiscal
fixation
flippant
foray
fusion

G
gamut
garish
garner
garnish
gauche
gird
gossamer
gradation
gratis
gregarious
guile

H
habituate
hackneyed
haggard
hallowed
harangue
harass
herbivorous
heresy
heretic
heterogeneous
hieroglyphics
homogeneous

equestrian
erode
estrange
ethereal
evince
exhort
exodus
exorbitant
expatriate
expedient
expound
extemporaneous
extol
extradition
extricate
exude

I
idiosyncrasy
ignoble
ignominious
illicit
imbibe
imbue
imminent
impasse
impeccable
impede
impel
impervious
impetuous
impetus
impotent
inalienable
incessant
incidence
incognito
incorrigible
incumbent
indefatigable
indemnity
indeterminate
indiscretion
indolent
indomitable
ineffectual
inexplicable
infamy
infectious
infinitesimal
infraction
ingenuous
ingratiate
inimitable
iniquity
innate
innuendo
inordinate
insatiable
insidious
insipid
intelligentsia
interminable
intrepid
intrinsic
inundate
invalidate
inveigle
inveterate
iridescent
itinerary

J
juncture
juxtaposition

EDL Reading Core Vocabulary—Graded Lists

L languid
languish
larceny
latent
laudable
lethargy
levity
lieu
limbo
lithe
longevity
lucrative
ludicrous
lurid

M macabre
magnanimous
magnate
manacle
marginal
maritime
maxim
median
mediation
mercenary
meritorious
metabolism
metamorphosis
meticulous
militant
misnomer
missive
modular
modulate
moot
motley
mundane

N nebulous
nomenclature
nondescript
nonentity
notoriety
novice
nuance
nuptial
nuture

O obesity
obsequious
obtuse
obviate
officiate
omnibus

omnipotent
omnivorous
opulent
orifice
orthodox
ostentatious
ostracize
overt

P pallid
panacea
pandemonium
paragon
paraphernalia
paraphrase
pariah
parlance
parody
pastoral
pathological
patriarch
patrician
pedagogy
penance
penitent
perfunctory
personify
pervade
perverse
pestilence
petulant
phlegmatic
pinion
piquant
pique
pirouette
pittance
plagiarize
plaintive
platitude
plaudit
plebeian
plummet
plurality
pneumatic
poignant
ponderous
posthumous
postulate
pragmatic
precedent
precept
preclude
precocious
predatory
predecessor
preeminent
prerogative
presentiment

pretentious
pretext
prevaricate
privation
procrastinate
prodigious
prodigy
proletariat
prolific
promiscuous
promissory
promontory
propagate
propitious
propound
prosaic
protégé
protocol
prototype
protract
prowess
proximity
pseudo
pseudonym
psyche
pungent
pursuant

Q quaff
quiescent
quintessence

R raiment
rancor
raze
recapitulate
recipient
recluse
recompense
recount
recrimination
redress
referendum
refraction
regale
regenerate
regurgitate
reiterate
relegate
relevant
remiss
reparation
repartée
replete
repository
reprobate
repudiate
repugnant

resilient
respite
restitution
resurgent
reticence
retrospect
reverberation
rhetoric
ribald
rudiment
ruminate

S sacrilege
sagacity
salient
salutary
sanctify
sardonic
scathing
scintillating
scion
secular
sedentary
senile
sinuous
solicitous
solstice
somnambulist
somnolent
sordid
soujourn
squalid
staid
stature
statute
stoic
subjugate
subservient
subsidiary
subsidy
subterfuge
succulent
succumb
suffused
sully
sumptuous
supercilious
supersede
supplant
supplication
surreptitious
surveillance
sustenance
sylvan
symposium

T taciturn
tantamount

tenacious
tenet
tertiary
tithe
tome
topography
tortuous
tractable
trajectory
transcend
transient
transitory
travesty
tremulous
trepidation
tutelage

U unwitting
upbraid
usurp
utilitarian

V vacillate
vapid
venerate
verdant
veritable
vernacular
vestige
vicarious
vindicate
vindictive
visage
vociferous
volatile
volition
voluble
voluminous
voluptuous
vulnerable

W wreak
wrest

Z zealous

EDL Reading Core Vocabulary—Graded Lists

Reading—13

A
abjure
ablution
abnegate
aborigine
abortive
abrogate
abstemious
abstruse
accede
accolade
accouterments
acquiesce
adjunct
adjure
adulation
adumbrate
alacrity
altercation
ambient
ambivalence
ameliorate
amnesty
amortize
anachronism
analogous
ancillary
anomaly
antipathy
antipodes
antithesis
aphorism
apocalyptic
apostasy
apotheosis
apprise
appurtenances
archaic
arrant
artifice
ascetic
asperity
assiduous
assuage
atavism
attest
auspicious
autonomous
avarice

B
baroque
bellicose
benighted
benign
blatant
bombast
bucolic

C
cacophonous
cairn
cajole
calligraphy
calumny
capacious
caprice
captious
carrion
cataclysm
catalepsy
caterwaul
certitude
chauvinism
chicanery
chimerical
choreography
circumspect
clandestine
clemency
cogent
cognizant
cohesive
collusion
comatose
commensurate
commiserate
commodious
concomitant
configuration
conjugal
connote
construe
consummate
contiguous
contingent
contrite
contumely
convivial
copious
corpulent
corroborate
coterie
covenant
covert
credence
culpable
cupidity
cursory
cynosure

D
dearth
debacle
debility
deciduous
decimate
declamation
declivity
decorum
defection
deficit
deleterious
demise
demur
denigrate
deprecate
desecrate
desiccate
diatribe
dichotomy
didactic
dilatory
dilettante
discomfiture
disparity
dissemble
dissident
dudgeon

E
ebullience
effete
efficacy
effusive
egregious
egress
elicit
elucidate
emolument
empirical
emulate
enamored
encomium
encroach
enervating
enigma
enmity
entity
entourage
entrepreneur
ephemeral
epicure
epilogue
epithet
epitome
equable
equanimity
equitable
equivocal
erudite
esoteric
etiology
eulogy
euphonious
evanescent
exacerbate
excoriate
execrate

exemplary
exigency
exonerate
expatiate
expiate
expostulate
expurge
extant
extenuating
extirpate

F
facile
factious
fallible
fatuous
fecund
fetish
filial
finite
flaccid
florid
flux
forensic
fortuitous
fractious
fruition

G
garrulous
gesticulate
glabrous
glaucous
gratuitous

H
halcyon
harbinger
hauteur
hegemony
heinous
hiatus
hierarchy
histrionic
homily
homonym
hyperbole

I
iconoclast
imbroglio
immutable
imperious
impious
implacable
implicit
importunate
imprecate

improvident
impunity
incarcerate
incarnate
inchoate
incipient
inclement
inculcate
indigenous
indigent
ineluctable
inexorable
inimical
innocuous
inscrutable
insouciance
insuperable
insurgent
intemperate
interim
interpolate
intransigence
inured
invective
invidious
irascible
irreparable
irrevocable
itinerant

J
jocund

L
laconic
laity
lassitude
lien
litigation
loquacious
lucid
lugubrious
luminary

M
machination
magniloquent
malevolent
malinger
martinet
masochistic
masticate
matriculate
matrix
maudlin
mellifluous
ménage
mendacity
milieu
millennium

EDL Reading Core Vocabulary—Graded Lists

misanthrope
miscegenation
miscreant
misogyny
mitigate
mollify
monolith
montage
moribund
munificent

N
necromancy
nefarious
nemesis
neophyte
nescience
noxious

O
obdurate
officious
oligarchy
omniscient
onerous
opiate
opprobrious
ostensible

P
palliative
palpable
pandemic
panegyric
paroxysm
parsimonious
parvenu
peccadillo
pecuniary
pedantic
penchant
penumbra
penury
peremptory
perfidious
peripatetic
permutation
pernicious
persiflage
perspicacious
philistine
philology
placate
plangent
plethora
polemic
polyglot
portend
precursor

predilection
prescience
pristine
probity
procreate
progeny
prolix
promulgate
propensity
propiquity
propitiate
protagonist
puerile
punctilious
pundit
purport
pusillanimous

Q
querulous
quixotic
quotidian

R
raconteur
rapacious
recalcitrant
recant
recondite
recumbent
refractory
remission
remonstrate
reprehensible
rescind
revile
rife
risible

S
salacious
salubrious
sanguine
sartorial
satiate
satrap
saturnine
schism
scurrilous
sedulous
sententious
servile
shibboleth
sinecure
soliloquy
sonorous
soporific
specious
sporadic
spurious

stentorian
stipend
strident
stringent
sublimate
succinct
succor
superannuated
supine
surfeit
sycophant
syllogism

T
tacit
temerity
terpsichorean
timorous
titular
torpid
transmute
trauma
travail
trenchant
truculent
truncheon
turgid

U
ubiquitous
umbrage
unction
unctuous
undulate
untrammeled
unwonted
usury
uxorious

V
vagary
variegated
vascular
vaunt
veracity
vernal
vertiginous
vested
vicissitude
virago
virulence
vitiate
vitriolic
voracious

X
xenophobia

Z
zealot

EDL Reading Core Vocabulary—Cumulative List

A

P a
9 a la carte
5 abandon
11 abashed
9 abate
8 abbreviate
8 abbreviation
11 abcess
11 abdicate
7 abdomen
12 abduct
12 aberration
12 abet
12 abeyance
9 abhor
5 ability
12 abject
13 abjure
2 able
13 ablution
13 abnegate
8 abnormal
3 aboard
8 abode
8 abolish
9 abolition
9 abominable
13 aborigine
13 abortive
9 abound
1 about
2 above
11 abrasion
11 abridge
7 abroad
13 abrogate
7 abrupt
6 absence
5 absent
9 absentee
7 absolute
6 absolutely
12 absolve
5 absorb
11 abstain
13 abstemious
12 abstinence
9 abstract
12 abstraction
13 abstruse
6 absurd
6 abundant
6 abuse
9 abyss
8 academic
5 academy
13 accede
8 accelerate
4 accent
10 accentuate

4 accept
8 acceptance
8 access
8 accessible
8 accessory
4 accident
6 accidentally
8 acclaim
12 acclimate
13 accolade
8 accommodate
8 accommodation
5 accompany
9 accomplice
6 accomplish
6 accomplishment
9 accord
4 according
6 accordion
11 accost
5 account
5 accounting
13 accouterments
12 accrue
8 accumulate
7 accuracy
6 accurate
9 accusation
4 accuse
6 accustomed
7 ace
4 ache
5 achieve
5 achievement
6 acid
7 acknowledge
7 acknowledgment
4 acorn
6 acquaint
6 acquaintance
13 acquiesce
6 acquire
11 acquisition
8 acquit
4 acre
8 acreage
11 acrid
12 acrimonious
4 acrobat
2 across
3 act
4 action
6 active
6 activity
4 actor
6 actress
7 actual
4 actually
8 actuate
12 acumen
7 acute

11 adage
12 adamant
5 adapt
9 adaptable
9 adaptation
3 add
11 addict
5 addition
6 additional
3 address
10 adept
8 adequate
9 adhere
12 adherent
7 adhesive
8 adjacent
7 adjoining
8 adjourn
13 adjunct
13 adjure
4 adjust
6 adjustment
9 administer
7 administration
8 admirable
5 admiral
5 admiration
4 admire
5 admission
4 admit
7 admittance
12 admonish
5 adobe
8 adolescent
5 adopt
6 adore
8 adorn
8 adrift
12 adroit
13 adulation
6 adult
11 adulterated
13 adumbrate
5 advance
7 advancement
5 advantage
12 advent
3 adventure
9 adversary
9 adverse
6 advertise
6 advertisement
6 advertising
5 advice
8 advisable
5 advise
8 adviser
8 advocate
7 aerial
7 aeronautics
12 aesthetic

11 affable
6 affair
5 affect
11 affectation
6 affection
7 affectionate
12 affidavit
12 affiliate
12 affinity
8 affirm
8 affirmative
11 affix
9 affliction
12 affluent
4 afford
10 affront
7 afloat
2 afraid
6 aft
1 after
11 aftermath
2 afternoon
5 afterward
1 again
3 against
3 age
7 aged
5 agent
8 aggravate
12 aggregate
11 aggression
9 aggressive
8 aghast
7 agile
9 agitate
12 agnostic
2 ago
7 agony
12 agrarian
4 agree
6 agreeable
6 agreement
5 agriculture
2 ahead
5 aid
8 aide
6 ailing
8 ailment
3 aim
2 air
6 aircraft
P airplane
3 airport
5 aisle
7 ajar
13 alacrity
3 alarm
6 alas
6 album
5 alcohol
8 alcoholic

9 alcove
6 alert
6 alfalfa
11 algae
7 algebra
7 alias
7 alibi
6 alien
11 alienate
11 align
3 alike
11 alimony
3 alive
1 all
8 allay
10 allay
12 allege
6 allegiance
12 allegory
11 alleviate
5 alley
7 alliance
4 alligator
12 allocate
9 allotment
3 allow
6 allowance
7 alloy
12 allude
10 allure
6 ally
7 almanac
2 almost
1 alone
1 along
8 aloof
4 alphabet
6 alphabetical
3 already
3 also
6 altar
5 alter
7 alteration
13 altercation
6 alternate
4 although
5 altitude
7 alto
4 altogether
12 altruistic
5 aluminum
11 alumni
2 always
5 A.M.
1 am
12 amalgamate
9 amass
6 amateur
3 amaze
6 amazement
8 ambassador

13 ambient
11 ambiguous
6 ambition
7 ambitious
13 ambivalence
6 ambulance
7 ambush
13 ameliorate
6 amen
12 amenable
7 amend
7 amendment
12 amenity
3 America
3 American
8 amiable
12 amicable
8 amid
12 amity
7 ammonia
5 ammunition
13 amnesty
3 among
12 amorphous
13 amortize
4 amount
8 amphibious
10 amphitheater
8 ample
9 amplify
11 amplitude
9 amputate
3 amuse
7 amusement
1 an
13 anachronism
13 analogous
11 analogy
9 analysis
8 analyze
12 anarchy
12 anathema
8 anatomy
4 ancestor
4 anchor
4 ancient
13 ancillary
P and
9 anecdote
8 anesthesia
8 anesthetic
11 anesthetic
5 angel
4 anger
5 angle
2 angry
7 anguish
1 animal
10 animation
12 animosity
5 ankle

─────────── EDL Reading Core Vocabulary—Cumulative List ───────────

11 annals	6 applaud	9 aroma	6 assistance
8 annex	6 applause	1 around	6 assistant
10 annihilate	1 apple	6 arouse	7 associate
7 anniversary	8 appliance	3 arrange	6 association
3 announce	8 applicant	4 arrangement	7 assortment
6 annoy	8 application	13 arrant	13 assuage
7 annoyance	6 apply	8 array	6 assume
6 annual	6 appoint	4 arrest	7 assurance
12 annuity	6 appointment	6 arrival	6 assure
10 annul	9 appraise	3 arrive	3 astonish
13 anomaly	5 appreciate	9 arrogant	5 astonishment
10 anonymous	5 appreciation	3 arrow	5 astound
1 another	9 apprehend	7 arsenal	12 astringent
2 answer	5 apprentice	8 arson	4 astronaut
3 ant	13 apprise	5 art	6 astronomer
9 antagonize	4 approach	8 artery	7 astronomy
11 antecedent	6 appropriate	9 artesian	12 astute
5 antelope	10 appropriation	5 artic	7 asylum
5 antenna	6 approval	4 article	P at
8 anthem	6 approve	9 articulate	13 atavism
8 anticipate	7 approximate	13 artifice	2 ate
8 antidote	7 approximately	6 artificial	11 atheist
13 antipathy	13 appurtenances	7 artillery	6 athlete
13 antipodes	5 apricot	10 artisan	5 athletic
11 antiquated	3 April	4 artist	7 atlas
6 antique	3 apron	1 as	5 atmosphere
8 antiseptic	7 apt	7 asbestos	6 atom
13 antithesis	9 aptitude	6 ascend	6 atomic
7 antler	6 aqualung	6 ascent	8 atone
5 anvil	4 aquarium	11 ascertain	10 atrocious
6 anxiety	9 aquatic	13 ascetic	12 atrophy
4 anxious	12 arable	11 ascribe	5 attach
1 any	9 arbitrary	4 ashamed	11 attache
4 anybody	11 arbitration	4 ashes	8 attachment
4 anyhow	7 arc	6 ashore	3 attack
2 anyone	5 arch	10 ashtray	6 attain
2 anything	6 archaeologist	1 ask	5 attempt
3 apart	13 archaic	12 askance	5 attend
2 apartment	7 archery	1 asked	5 attendance
12 apathy	6 architect	11 askew	6 attendant
5 ape	6 architecture	2 asleep	4 attention
11 aperture	12 archives	8 aspect	8 attentive
10 apex	8 ardent	13 asperity	13 attest
13 aphorism	10 ardor	12 aspersion	4 attic
13 apocalyptic	12 arduous	6 asphalt	6 attire
5 apologize	1 are	11 asphyxiation	6 attitude
7 apology	4 area	11 aspiration	8 attorney
13 apostasy	6 arena	11 assail	5 attract
13 apotheosis	3 aren't	7 assassinate	7 attraction
10 appalling	4 argue	7 assault	6 attractive
7 apparatus	6 argument	6 assemble	9 attribute
8 apparel	9 arid	7 assembly	6 auction
6 apparently	8 aristocrat	9 assent	12 audacity
12 apparition	4 arithmetic	8 assert	9 audible
5 appeal	2 arm	10 assess	5 audience
3 appear	8 armament	9 asset	11 audit
4 appearance	6 armistice	13 assiduous	9 audition
8 appease	5 armor	6 assign	5 auditorium
7 appendicitis	7 armory	6 assignment	10 auditory
7 appendix	9 armory	11 assimilate	12 augment
5 appetite	3 army	6 assist	4 August

1 aunt	1 bag
10 aura	3 baggage
13 auspicious	7 bail
12 austerity	3 bait
8 authentic	2 bake
6 author	4 balance
6 authority	5 balcony
8 authorize	6 bald
9 autobiography	5 bale
12 autocracy	12 baleful
5 autograph	7 balk
5 automatic	P ball
10 automation	7 ballad
3 automobile	8 ballast
13 autonomous	7 ballet
3 autumn	1 balloon
8 auxiliary	6 ballot
9 avail	7 balm
6 available	4 bamboo
6 avalanche	7 ban
13 avarice	12 banal
6 avenge	3 banana
4 avenue	2 band
3 average	4 bandage
11 aversion	8 bandanna
9 avert	5 bandit
6 aviation	10 bane
6 aviator	2 bang
12 avid	7 banish
12 avocation	9 banister
4 avoid	5 banjo
7 await	2 bank
3 awake	8 bankrupt
5 award	4 banner
5 aware	6 banquet
P away	10 banter
6 awe	7 baptize
3 awful	3 bar
4 awkward	6 barb
7 awning	8 barbarian
4 awoke	7 barbecue
11 awry	6 barber
3 ax	4 bare
10 axiom	6 barely
6 axis	3 bargain
6 axle	6 barge
4 aye	2 bark
	5 barley
B	1 barn
2 babies	8 barnacle
1 baby	7 barometer
7 bachelor	6 baron
1 back	13 baroque
6 backward	9 barracks
4 bacon	3 barrel
5 bacteria	6 barren
2 bad	8 barricade
6 bade	7 barrier
4 badge	5 barter
6 badger	3 base
7 baffle	3 baseball

EDL Reading Core Vocabulary—Cumulative List

4 basement	7 begrudge	4 bid	5 blond	5 bough	7 brittle
7 bashful	12 beguile	8 bide	3 blood	2 bought	11 broach
7 basic	3 begun	11 biennial	5 bloom	2 bought	5 broad
5 basin	6 behalf	11 bier	3 blossom	5 boulder	6 broadcast
7 basis	3 behave	P big	6 blot	7 boulevard	6 broil
7 bask	5 behavior	2 bigger	8 blotter	2 bounce	3 broke
1 basket	1 behind	2 biggest	6 blouse	4 bound	2 broken
2 basketball	6 behold	12 bigot	2 blow	6 boundary	8 broker
6 bass	9 beige	4 bike	4 blubber	6 bounty	5 bronze
9 baste	1 being	11 bilingual	P blue	5 bouquet	6 brood
2 bat	10 belated	2 bill	3 blueberry	12 bourgeois	3 brook
7 batch	7 belfry	9 billiards	5 bluff	8 bout	4 broom
3 bath	10 belie	6 billion	5 blunder	3 bow	7 broth
5 bathe	6 belief	4 billow	7 blunt	3 bowl	2 brother
4 bathroom	2 believe	5 bin	5 blur	1 box	6 brow
4 bathtub	7 belittle	5 bind	5 blush	1 boy	1 brown
6 baton	2 bell	11 binder	2 board	11 boycott	4 brownie
8 battalion	13 bellicose	8 binoculars	8 boarder	5 brace	8 browse
3 batter	9 belligerent	7 biography	3 boast	4 bracelet	4 bruise
4 battery	4 bellows	10 biology	1 boat	7 bracket	8 brunt
4 battle	6 belly	4 birch	4 bob	5 brag	3 brush
10 bauble	2 belong	1 bird	3 body	4 braid	11 brusque
4 bay	6 beloved	3 birth	5 bog	4 brain	7 brutal
9 bayonet	3 below	1 birthday	10 bogus	5 brake	7 brute
6 bazaar	3 belt	6 biscuit	3 boil	2 branch	3 bubble
1 be	3 bench	6 bishop	6 boiler	5 brand	4 buck
3 beach	3 bend	2 bit	10 boisterous	10 brandish	3 bucket
6 beacon	4 beneath	2 bite	3 bold	4 brass	4 buckle
3 bead	9 benediction	5 bitter	10 bolster	2 brave	13 bucolic
4 beak	10 benefactor	11 bizarre	5 bolt	8 bravery	5 bud
4 beam	8 beneficial	1 black	5 bomb	8 brawl	5 budge
3 bean	11 beneficiary	7 blackmail	7 bombard	8 brawn	8 budget
1 bear	5 benefit	6 blacksmith	13 bombast	9 brazen	3 buffalo
3 beard	10 benevolent	3 blade	6 bond	8 breach	9 buffer
3 beast	13 benighted	4 blame	8 bondage	2 bread	7 buffet
3 beat	13 benign	10 bland	2 bone	8 breadth	3 bug
7 beau	3 bent	5 blank	5 bonfire	2 break	4 buggy
2 beautiful	11 bequeath	3 blanket	4 bonnet	2 breakfast	5 bugle
3 beauty	10 bereaved	8 blare	7 bonus	6 breast	2 build
3 beaver	2 berry	12 blasphemy	1 book	3 breath	2 building
7 becalm	5 berth	3 blast	5 bookkeeper	4 breathe	3 built
3 became	7 beseech	13 blatant	6 boom	8 bred	3 bulb
2 because	2 beside	4 blaze	7 boomerang	5 breeches	4 bulge
6 beckon	8 besiege	9 bleach	8 boon	5 breed	6 bulk
3 become	1 best	7 bleak	6 boost	3 breeze	3 bull
1 bed	9 bestow	4 bleat	3 boot	11 brevity	6 bulldozer
10 bedlam	4 bet	6 bleed	5 booth	7 brew	4 bullet
3 bedroom	6 betray	8 blemish	9 booty	7 bribe	6 bulletin
1 bee	10 betroth	4 blend	5 border	3 brick	5 bully
6 beech	1 better	3 bless	5 bore	5 bride	11 bulwark
4 beef	2 between	3 blessing	8 boredom	2 bridge	6 bumper
3 beehive	10 bevel	2 blew	3 born	5 bridle	4 bun
2 been	8 beverage	8 blight	8 borne	6 brief	3 bunch
4 beetle	10 bevy	3 blind	3 borrow	6 brier	3 bundle
5 beets	6 beware	7 blindfold	9 bosom	8 brigade	7 bungalow
10 befall	5 bewilder	4 blink	5 boss	2 bright	3 bunk
1 before	9 bewitch	7 bliss	11 botany	5 brilliant	7 bunt
3 beg	3 beyond	5 blister	2 both	6 brim	5 buoy
1 began	8 bias	4 blizzard	3 bother	1 bring	8 buoyancy
6 beggar	5 Bible	8 bloated	2 bottle	8 brink	5 burden
2 begin	9 bibliography	2 block	2 bottom	5 brisk	6 bureau
2 beginning	2 bicycle	7 blockade	11 boudoir	7 bristle	12 bureaucracy

EDL Reading Core Vocabulary—Cumulative List

5 burglar	4 calves	3 cardboard	6 caution	4 charcoal	3 chop
7 burial	1 came	2 care	5 cautious	3 charge	8 choral
7 burlap	5 camel	8 careen	11 cavalcade	7 chariot	6 chord
11 burlesque	3 camera	6 career	8 cavalry	6 charity	4 chore
2 burn	8 camouflage	2 careful	3 cave	12 charlatan	13 choreography
11 burnish	2 camp	3 careless	7 cavern	5 charm	5 chorus
5 burnt	6 campaign	8 caress	7 cavity	5 chart	3 chose
7 burr	7 campus	4 cargo	6 cease	8 charter	4 chosen
4 burro	P can	6 caribou	5 cedar	2 chase	8 chowder
4 burrow	5 canal	11 caricature	12 cede	7 chasm	2 Christmas
4 burst	3 canary	7 carload	5 ceiling	8 chassis	8 chromium
4 bury	7 cancel	12 carnage	4 celebrate	12 chaste	10 chronic
1 bus	10 cancellation	7 carnation	5 celebration	12 chasten	3 chuckle
2 bush	7 cancer	4 carnival	9 celebrity	12 chastise	5 chum
4 bushel	11 candid	10 carnivorous	6 celery	6 chat	5 chunk
4 business	6 candidate	3 carol	11 celestial	12 chattel	3 church
6 bust	2 candle	11 carouse	5 cell	3 chatter	4 churn
5 bustle	12 candor	4 carpenter	3 cellar	7 chauffeur	6 chute
2 busy	2 candy	3 carpet	5 cement	13 chauvinism	6 cider
1 but	4 cane	4 carriage	6 cemetery	5 cheap	6 cigar
3 butcher	10 canine	2 carried	8 censor	5 cheat	6 cigarette
6 butler	7 cannibal	13 carrion	12 censure	4 check	5 cinder
5 butt	3 cannon	3 carrot	8 census	5 checker	9 cinema
2 butter	2 cannot	2 carry	2 cent	3 cheek	7 cinnamon
3 butterfly	3 canoe	3 cart	10 centennial	3 cheer	3 circle
2 button	6 canopy	6 carton	3 center	4 cheerful	8 circuit
10 buttress	1 can't	6 cartoon	5 central	3 cheese	6 circular
1 buy	7 cantaloupe	7 cartridge	11 centrifugal	7 chef	7 circulate
7 buzzard	12 cantankerous	3 carve	5 century	5 chemical	7 circumference
1 by	7 canteen	8 cascade	5 cereal	6 chemist	13 circumspect
	4 canvas	3 case	12 cerebral	5 chemistry	9 circumstance
C	9 canvass	6 cash	5 ceremony	7 cherish	7 circumstances
5 cab	4 canyon	7 cashier	3 certain	3 cherry	12 circumvent
4 cabbage	2 cap	5 cask	3 certainly	7 chess	1 circus
3 cabin	6 capable	6 casket	5 certificate	3 chest	8 cistern
5 cabinet	13 capacious	8 casserole	8 certify	3 chew	12 citation
4 cable	6 capacity	4 cast	13 certitude	13 chicanery	11 cite
8 cache	5 cape	12 caste	11 cessation	3 chick	4 citizen
13 cacophonous	9 caper	4 castle	9 chafe	2 chicken	6 citizenship
5 cactus	10 capillary	5 casual	10 chagrin	9 chide	2 city
12 cadaverous	5 capital	8 casualty	3 chain	3 chief	7 civic
7 caddie	11 capitalist	1 cat	2 chair	3 child	7 civics
6 cadet	9 capitalize	13 cataclysm	7 chairman	6 childhood	5 civil
5 cafe	5 capitol	13 catalepsy	5 chalk	1 children	8 civilian
5 cafeteria	12 capitulate	6 catalog	5 challenge	5 chill	6 civilization
2 cage	13 caprice	8 catapult	5 chamber	5 chilly	5 civilized
13 cairn	8 capsize	11 cataract	9 champagne	8 chime	6 clad
13 cajole	5 capsule	9 catastrophe	4 champion	13 chimerical	4 claim
1 cake	3 captain	1 catch	3 chance	2 chimney	11 claimant
8 calamity	9 caption	11 catechism	2 change	4 chimpanzee	4 clam
7 calculate	13 captious	9 category	7 changeable	3 chin	6 clamber
3 calendar	9 captivate	10 cater	5 channel	4 china	8 clamor
1 calf	5 captive	6 caterpillar	5 chant	2 chip	6 clamp
9 caliber	9 captivity	13 caterwaul	5 chaos	2 chipmunk	7 clan
6 calico	4 capture	6 cathedral	6 chap	6 chirp	13 clandestine
1 call	P car	6 catsup	7 chapel	5 chisel	3 clap
1 called	10 carat	3 cattle	8 chaplain	7 chivalry	8 clarify
13 calligraphy	5 caravan	12 caucus	5 chapter	3 chocolate	6 clasp
10 callous	6 carbon	2 caught	8 char	5 choice	3 class
3 calm	8 carburetor	9 cauldron	4 character	5 choir	8 classic
8 calorie	7 carcass	3 cause	6 characteristic	4 choke	8 classification
13 calumny	2 card	12 caustic	12 characterize	3 choose	8 classify

EDL Reading Core Vocabulary—Cumulative List

4 clatter	13 cogent	6 commission	7 conceit	12 conjecture	11 context
7 clause	12 cogitate	7 commit	7 conceive	13 conjugal	13 contiguous
4 claw	13 cognizant	4 committee	5 concentrate	5 connect	4 continent
4 clay	12 coherent	13 commodious	12 concentric	6 connection	13 contingent
2 clean	13 cohesive	9 commodity	10 concept	12 connive	6 continual
8 cleanse	12 cohort	3 common	11 conception	12 connoisseur	3 continue
3 clear	5 coil	7 commotion	5 concern	13 connote	9 continuity
8 clearance	4 coin	12 communal	5 concert	5 conquer	7 continuous
9 cleave	9 coincide	11 commune	9 concession	6 conquest	11 contortion
13 clemency	8 coincidence	10 communicable	12 conciliate	6 conscience	9 contour
5 clench	1 cold	6 communicate	9 concise	9 conscientious	10 contraband
8 clergy	11 collaborate	6 communication	12 conclave	5 conscious	6 contract
9 clerical	7 collapse	8 communism	6 conclude	12 conscription	9 contraction
5 clerk	4 collar	5 community	6 conclusion	11 consecrate	8 contradict
2 clever	12 collateral	9 commute	10 conclusive	9 consecutive	6 contraption
6 click	10 colleague	5 compact	11 concoct	12 consensus	6 contrary
8 client	4 collect	4 companion	13 concomitant	5 consent	7 contrast
10 clientele	4 collection	3 company	12 concourse	8 consequence	6 contribute
3 cliff	11 collective	9 comparable	5 concrete	8 consequently	13 contrite
4 climate	5 college	10 comparative	11 concur	6 conservation	12 contrive
7 climax	10 collegiate	5 compare	11 concussion	9 conservative	4 control
2 climb	8 collide	6 comparison	6 condemn	5 consider	8 controversy
5 cling	5 collie	7 compartment	5 condense	6 considerable	13 contumely
8 clinic	8 collision	5 compass	11 condescend	7 considerate	10 convalescent
3 clip	12 colloquial	11 compassion	11 condiment	6 consideration	12 convene
9 clique	13 collusion	11 compatible	4 condition	6 consist	4 convenience
5 cloak	4 colonel	7 compel	8 conditional	8 consistent	4 convenient
2 clock	5 colonial	9 compensation	11 condolence	8 consolation	5 convention
8 clog	5 colonist	7 compete	11 condone	8 console	9 conventional
2 close	4 colony	8 competent	6 conduct	10 consolidate	9 converge
3 closet	1 color	7 competition	11 conductive	8 conspicuous	12 conversant
7 clot	7 colossal	10 compile	3 conductor	8 conspiracy	5 conversation
3 cloth	3 colt	11 complacent	4 cone	8 constable	11 converse
2 clothes	5 column	3 complain	11 confection	6 constant	9 conversion
3 clothing	8 columnist	6 complaint	8 confederate	9 constellation	8 convert
3 cloud	8 coma	10 complement	11 confederation	12 constituent	9 convertible
4 clover	13 comatose	3 complete	8 confer	11 constitute	11 convex
1 clown	3 comb	9 complex	6 conference	6 constitution	7 convey
3 club	6 combat	7 complexion	5 confess	12 constraint	10 conveyance
5 clue	6 combination	7 complicate	8 confetti	5 construct	7 conveyor
4 clump	6 combine	12 complicity	12 confidant	5 construction	8 convict
5 clumsy	9 combustion	5 compliment	5 confide	13 construe	7 conviction
5 clung	P come	9 comply	5 confidence	8 consul	5 convince
5 cluster	8 comedian	10 component	5 confident	5 consult	13 convivial
5 clutch	7 comedy	6 compose	8 confidential	10 consultant	8 convoy
8 clutter	12 comely	11 composite	13 configuration	7 consume	10 convulsion
3 coach	7 comet	5 composition	6 confine	7 consumer	2 cook
2 coal	4 comfort	11 composure	8 confirm	13 consummate	1 cookie
5 coarse	3 comfortable	6 compound	9 confiscate	6 contact	3 cool
3 coast	6 comic	8 comprehend	6 conflict	7 contagious	7 coop
1 coat	1 coming	9 compress	8 conform	4 contain	5 cooperate
4 coax	4 command	12 comprise	10 confound	8 contaminate	7 cooperative
4 cobbler	11 commemorate	7 compromise	7 confront	9 contemplate	9 coordination
6 cockpit	6 commence	10 compulsion	5 confuse	9 contemporary	8 cope
4 cocoa	9 commend	9 compulsory	6 confusion	8 contempt	13 copious
3 coconut	13 commensurate	9 compute	11 congeal	10 contemptible	3 copper
5 cocoon	5 comment	8 computer	11 congenial	11 contemptuous	3 copy
5 code	11 commentary	5 comrade	9 congestion	11 contend	8 copyright
12 coerce	7 commerce	11 concave	5 congratulate	3 content	4 coral
3 coffee	6 commercial	6 conceal	9 congregation	6 contents	4 cord
7 coffin	13 commiserate	9 concede	5 congress	3 contest	7 cordial
7 cog			9 contestant		

47

EDL Reading Core Vocabulary—Cumulative List

6 core	2 cover	6 critical	8 currency
4 cork	13 covert	7 criticism	4 current
2 corn	11 covet	6 criticize	10 curriculum
2 corner	1 cow	9 crochet	8 curry
12 corollary	3 coward	4 crocodile	6 curse
9 coronation	9 cower	4 crooked	13 cursory
10 coroner	8 coy	4 crop	10 curtail
8 corporal	4 coyote	7 croquet	3 curtain
8 corporation	3 cozy	2 cross	6 curtsy
6 corps	4 crab	4 crouch	10 curvature
7 corpse	3 crack	2 crow	4 curve
13 corpulent	5 crackle	3 crowd	6 cushion
4 corral	5 cradle	3 crown	5 custard
3 correct	5 craft	10 crucial	9 custodian
5 correction	4 crag	5 crude	8 custody
12 correlate	7 cram	4 cruel	4 custom
6 correspond	9 cram	8 cruelty	6 customary
7 correspondence	6 cramp	6 cruise	4 customer
6 correspondent	5 cranberry	4 crumb	2 cut
6 corridor	5 crane	5 crumble	4 cute
13 corroborate	5 crank	6 crumple	10 cuticle
8 corrode	3 crash	6 crunch	8 cutlery
9 corrugated	12 crass	7 crusade	2 cutting
8 corrupt	6 crate	5 crush	6 cycle
9 cosmetics	5 crater	5 crust	6 cyclone
10 cosmic	9 crave	6 crutch	6 cylinder
11 cosmopolitan	2 crawl	1 cry	10 cynical
3 cost	4 crayon	10 crypt	13 cynosure
6 costly	4 crazy	10 cryptic	6 cypress
3 costume	4 creak	5 crystal	11 cyst
4 cot	2 cream	4 cub	
13 coterie	7 crease	6 cube	
4 cottage	6 create	6 cubic	
4 cotton	9 creation	6 cuddle	
6 couch	7 creative	7 cue	
6 cougar	4 creature	6 cuff	
5 cough	13 credence	11 cuisine	
1 could	10 credentials	11 culinary	
2 couldn't	12 credible	10 cull	
4 council	5 credit	12 culminate	
6 counsel	10 creditor	13 culpable	
2 count	12 credulous	8 culprit	
9 countenance	7 creed	9 cult	
4 counter	3 creek	6 cultivate	
9 counteract	4 creep	7 cultural	
8 counterfeit	3 crept	7 culture	
2 country	9 crescent	8 cumbersome	
5 county	5 crest	10 cumulative	
7 coupé	7 crevice	6 cunning	
4 couple	4 crew	3 cup	
6 coupon	4 crib	4 cupboard	
3 courage	4 cricket	13 cupidity	
6 courageous	2 cried	5 curb	
10 courier	5 crime	8 curdle	
3 course	6 criminal	4 cure	
4 court	7 crimson	8 curfew	
6 courteous	4 cripple	7 curio	
6 courtesy	6 crisis	4 curiosity	
8 courtship	4 crisp	3 curious	
3 cousin	6 crisscross	3 curl	
4 cove	11 criterion	4 curly	
13 covenant	7 critic		

D

2 dad	3 dawn	2 deer
P daddy	1 day	9 deface
6 dagger	6 daze	10 default
5 daily	5 dazzle	5 defeat
10 daily	3 dead	8 defect
5 dainty	5 deaf	13 defection
4 dairy	5 deafen	8 defective
4 daisy	4 deal	4 defend
5 dam	7 dealer	8 defendant
4 damage	7 dealt	6 defense
9 damnable	9 dean	9 defensive
3 damp	2 dear	11 defer
2 dance	13 dearth	12 deference
6 dandelion	4 death	7 defiance
4 dandy	13 debacle	10 deficient
3 danger	12 debase	13 deficit
4 dangerous	9 debatable	10 defile
4 dangle	6 debate	7 define
3 dare	13 debility	6 definite
1 dark	10 debit	6 definition
3 darkness	11 debonair	12 definitive
5 darling	8 debris	8 deflate
5 darn	4 debt	10 deflation
5 dart	7 debtor	8 deflect
3 dash	10 debutante	8 deformity
9 data	8 decade	12 defray
4 date	12 decadence	7 defrost
3 daughter	6 decay	10 deft
9 dauntless	9 deceased	12 defunct
	8 deceit	6 defy
	6 deceive	12 degenerate
	4 December	4 degree
	6 decent	12 deify
	8 deception	10 deity
	3 decide	9 dejected
	13 deciduous	5 delay
	6 decimal	6 delegate
	13 decimate	9 delete
	8 deciper	13 deleterious
	5 decision	9 deliberate
	9 decisive	5 delicate
	3 deck	8 delicatessen
	13 declamation	3 delicious
	5 declaration	3 delight
	4 declare	12 delineation
	6 decline	9 delinquent
	13 declivity	8 delirious
	8 decompose	4 deliver
	4 decorate	4 delivery
	6 decoration	12 delude
	13 decorum	8 deluge
	7 decoy	12 delusion
	5 decrease	10 delve
	5 decree	12 demagogue
	11 decrepit	4 demand
	12 decry	12 demeanor
	6 dedicate	10 demented
	8 deduct	7 demerit
	4 deed	13 demise
	9 deem	6 democracy
	2 deep	7 Democrat

EDL Reading Core Vocabulary—Cumulative List

6 democratic
8 demolish
10 demolition
6 demon
5 demonstrate
10 demoralize
13 demur
10 demure
4 den
8 denial
13 denigrate
8 denim
9 denomination
12 denote
9 denounce
5 dense
9 density
5 dent
8 dental
5 dentist
5 deny
7 depart
4 department
6 departure
3 depend
7 dependent
10 dependent
11 depict
11 deplete
9 deplore
8 deport
6 deposit
5 depot
12 depraved
13 deprecate
10 depreciate
8 depress
8 depression
8 deprive
6 depth
7 deputy
11 derange
7 derby
11 derelict
12 deride
12 derivative
8 derive
6 derrick
5 descend
5 descendant
7 descent
5 describe
6 description
13 desecrate
3 desert
9 desertion
3 deserve
13 desiccate
4 design
10 designate
7 desirable

5 desire
11 desirous
12 desist
3 desk
7 desolate
6 despair
5 desperate
12 despicable
7 despise
7 despite
10 despondent
12 despot
4 dessert
6 destination
7 destiny
9 destitute
4 destroy
6 destruction
12 desultory
9 detach
5 detail
8 detain
7 detect
4 detective
9 detention
11 deter
10 deteriorate
6 determination
5 determine
8 detest
12 detonate
6 detour
9 detract
11 detriment
10 devastate
4 develop
7 development
11 deviate
5 device
6 devil
11 devious
7 devise
11 devoid
6 devote
6 devotion
6 devour
8 devout
5 dew
11 dexterity
11 diagnosis
6 diagonal
6 diagram
5 dial
10 dialect
7 dialogue
6 diameter
3 diamond
7 diaper
10 diaphragm
6 diary
13 diatribe

6 dice
13 dichotomy
8 dictate
8 dictator
9 diction
4 dictionary
P did
13 didactic
2 didn't
3 die
5 diesel
6 diet
6 differ
3 difference
2 different
11 differential
12 differentiate
4 difficult
12 diffident
11 diffuse
2 dig
7 digest
7 digestion
6 dignified
10 dignitary
4 dignity
12 digression
5 dike
11 dilapidated
10 dilate
13 dilatory
10 dilemma
13 dilettante
10 diligent
8 dilute
4 dim
3 dime
8 dimension
8 diminish
12 diminutive
7 dimple
8 din
3 dine
8 dingy
2 dinner
4 dinosaur
3 dip
8 diploma
9 diplomacy
8 diplomat
5 diptheria
9 dire
4 direct
3 direction
7 director
7 directory
10 dirge
8 dirigible
3 dirt
2 dirty
7 disable

7 disagree
7 disagreeable
3 disappear
3 disappoint
4 disappointment
9 disapprove
7 disarm
5 disaster
9 disastrous
9 disband
9 disbelief
7 discard
11 discern
8 discharge
9 disciple
8 discipline
9 disclose
13 discomfiture
9 discomfort
10 disconcert
9 disconnect
12 disconsolate
9 discontent
9 discontinue
9 discord
7 discount
6 discourage
11 discourse
3 discover
4 discovery
11 discredit
12 discreet
11 discrepancy
10 discretion
8 discriminate
5 discuss
6 discussion
6 disdain
11 disdainful
4 disease
9 disembark
9 disengage
9 disfigure
11 disgorge
4 disgrace
5 disguise
4 disgust
2 dish
11 disheveled
7 dishonest
8 dishonor
10 disillusion
7 disinfectant
8 disinherit
10 disintegrate
6 disk
6 dislike
8 dislocate
8 dislodge
6 dismal
9 dismantle

4 dismay
5 dismiss
7 disobey
7 disorder
9 disorganized
7 disown
12 disparage
13 disparity
8 dispatch
10 dispel
10 dispensary
8 dispense
10 dispense
11 disperse
8 displace
10 displacement
6 display
7 displease
5 dispose
6 disposition
9 dispossess
11 disproportionate
8 disprove
6 dispute
9 disqualify
8 disregard
10 disreputable
8 disrespect
9 disrupt
8 dissatisfied
10 dissect
13 dissemble
12 disseminate
12 dissent
12 dissertation
13 dissident
11 dissimilar
12 dissipate
11 dissociate
6 dissolve
12 dissonant
12 dissuade
4 distance
4 distant
9 distasteful
12 distend
6 distinct
7 distinction
6 distinguish
6 distinguished
8 distort
6 distract
11 distraught
5 distress
6 distribute
8 distribution
5 district
6 distrust
4 disturb
6 disturbance
10 disuse

5 ditch
3 dive
9 diverge
10 diverse
9 diversion
9 divert
3 divide
8 dividend
7 divine
5 division
8 divorce
9 divulge
5 dizzy
P do
11 docile
4 dock
3 doctor
8 doctrine
6 document
5 dodge
4 doe
1 does
3 doesn't
9 doff
1 dog
10 dogged
5 dogie
12 dogmatic
1 doing
11 doleful
1 doll
2 dollar
9 domain
6 dome
7 domestic
12 domicile
10 dominant
8 dominate
5 dominoes
7 donate
7 donation
2 done
2 donkey
7 donor
1 don't
6 doom
1 door
10 dormant
7 dormitory
6 dose
5 dot
10 dote
5 double
4 doubt
7 doubtful
8 doubtless
5 dough
5 doughnut
8 douse
5 dove
P down

49

EDL Reading Core Vocabulary—Cumulative List

3 downstairs	6 duet	10 economize	8 eliminate
9 dowry	3 dug	8 economy	12 elixir
6 doze	5 duke	9 ecstasy	6 elk
4 dozen	4 dull	11 eddy	11 elliptical
3 Dr.	9 duly	2 edge	5 elm
8 drab	3 dumb	8 edible	10 elongate
6 draft	6 dummy	12 edict	7 elope
3 drag	5 dump	12 ediface	10 eloquent
4 dragon	5 dune	8 edit	2 else
5 drain	6 dungeon	6 edition	13 elucidate
7 drama	10 dupe	4 editor	8 elude
7 dramatic	8 duplicate	8 editorial	3 elves
3 drank	12 duplicity	5 educate	11 emaciated
6 drape	6 durable	5 education	12 emanate
7 drapery	8 duration	6 eel	10 emancipate
8 drastic	12 duress	4 effect	8 emancipation
3 draw	3 during	7 effective	9 embalm
3 drawer	5 dusk	12 effervescence	6 embankment
8 drawl	3 dust	13 effete	8 embargo
4 drawn	9 dutiful	13 efficacy	5 embarrass
5 dread	4 duty	8 efficiency	7 embarrassment
4 dreadful	5 dwarf	7 efficient	8 embassy
3 dream	7 dwell	12 effigy	10 embellish
5 dreary	6 dwelling	5 effort	6 ember
8 dredge	9 dwindle	12 effrontery	9 embezzle
10 dregs	5 dye	13 effusive	6 emblem
6 drench	10 dynamic	1 egg	12 embody
1 dress	5 dynamite	11 egotism	10 emboss
5 dresser	11 dynasty	13 egregious	8 embrace
3 drew		13 egress	5 embroider
3 dried	**E**	2 eight	12 embroiled
3 drift	1 each	4 eighteen	10 embryo
5 drill	3 eager	4 eighth	8 emerald
2 drink	3 eagle	3 eighty	6 emerge
3 drip	2 ear	3 either	5 emergency
2 drive	2 early	8 eject	8 emigrant
2 driver	3 earn	6 elaborate	8 emigrate
10 droll	4 earnest	8 elapse	11 eminent
11 drone	8 earshot	6 elastic	10 emit
4 droop	3 earth	8 elated	13 emolument
2 drop	4 earthquake	5 elbow	8 emotion
5 drought	9 earthy	6 elder	5 emperor
3 drove	5 ease	5 elect	8 emphasis
2 drown	5 easel	5 election	7 emphasize
5 drowsy	3 easily	12 electorate	11 emphatic
9 drudgery	3 east	4 electric	6 empire
6 drug	4 Easter	4 electricity	13 empirical
6 druggist	4 eastern	8 electrocute	6 employ
3 drum	2 easy	5 electronic	6 employee
5 drunk	1 eat	4 elegant	6 employer
8 drunkard	8 eaves	11 elegy	6 employment
3 dry	9 ebb	6 element	2 empty
7 dual	7 ebony	6 elementary	13 emulate
12 dub	13 ebullience	2 elephant	6 enable
11 dubious	10 eccentric	7 elevate	8 enact
6 duchess	12 ecclesiastical	6 elevation	5 enamel
1 duck	12 echelon	2 elevator	13 enamored
10 duct	4 echo	3 eleven	10 encampment
13 dudgeon	8 eclipse	3 elf	6 enchant
5 due	8 economical	13 elicit	8 encircle
6 duel	6 economics	8 eligible	5 enclose
5 dues			

8 enclosure	13 entourage
13 encomium	5 entrance
8 encompass	12 entreat
9 encore	13 entrepreneur
8 encounter	9 entrust
4 encourage	6 entry
13 encroach	10 enumerate
11 encumbered	10 enunciate
4 encyclopedia	8 envelop
2 end	4 envelope
8 endanger	9 enviable
9 endear	8 envious
8 endeavor	7 environment
8 endorse	9 envoy
8 endow	5 envy
4 endurance	13 ephemeral
6 endure	11 epic
4 enemy	13 epicure
8 energetic	8 epidemic
6 energy	13 epilogue
13 enervating	8 episode
8 enfold	11 epitaph
7 enforce	13 epithet
6 engage	13 epitome
2 engine	12 epoch
4 engineer	13 equable
3 English	4 equal
7 engrave	8 equality
11 engross	13 equanimity
10 enhance	4 equator
13 enigma	12 equestrian
3 enjoy	10 equilibrium
7 enlarge	5 equip
10 enlighten	5 equipment
7 enlist	13 equitable
11 enliven	11 equity
13 enmity	9 equivalent
4 enormous	13 equivocal
2 enough	7 era
6 enrage	10 eradicate
10 enrapture	5 erase
8 enrich	5 eraser
7 enroll	6 erect
8 enrollment	12 erode
12 ensconced	6 erosion
10 ensemble	9 err
11 ensue	5 errand
11 entail	11 erratic
8 entangle	11 erroneous
3 enter	6 error
5 enterprise	13 erudite
5 entertain	7 erupt
5 entertainment	8 escalator
10 enthrall	9 escapade
6 enthusiasm	3 escape
7 enthusiastic	6 escort
9 entice	4 Eskimo
4 entire	13 esoteric
5 entirely	4 especially
7 entitle	9 espionage
13 entity	6 essay

_____ **EDL Reading Core Vocabulary—Cumulative List** _____

11 essence	3 exclaim	5 export	4 factory
6 essential	8 exclamation	6 expose	8 faculty
5 establish	8 exclude	8 exposition	7 fad
6 estate	8 exclusive	13 expostulate	4 fade
10 esteem	13 excoriate	7 exposure	3 fail
6 estimate	11 excruciating	12 expound	5 failure
12 estrange	7 excursion	4 express	3 faint
6 etc.	3 excuse	5 expression	2 fair
7 eternal	13 execrate	10 expressly	2 fairy
7 eternity	6 execute	11 expulsion	5 faith
12 ethereal	7 executive	13 expurge	3 faithful
10 ethical	13 exemplary	8 exquisite	6 fake
13 etiology	8 exempt	13 extant	2 fall
8 etiquette	3 exercise	12 extemporaneous	10 fallacy
13 eulogy	6 exert	5 extend	13 fallible
13 euphonious	7 exhale	8 extension	11 fallow
8 evacuate	5 exhaust	6 extent	6 false
8 evade	5 exhausted	13 extenuating	7 falsehood
10 evaluate	5 exhaustion	8 exterior	7 falter
13 evanescent	5 exhibit	9 exterminate	5 fame
6 evaporate	5 exhibition	8 external	4 familiar
10 evasion	11 exhilarated	8 extinct	2 family
8 evasive	12 exhort	8 extinguish	7 famine
4 eve	13 exigency	13 extirpate	9 famished
2 even	7 exile	12 extol	3 famous
2 evening	6 exist	11 extortion	3 fan
3 event	6 existence	3 extra	8 fanatic
6 eventual	6 exit	8 extract	3 fancy
2 ever	12 exodus	12 extradition	6 fang
1 every	13 exonerate	8 extraordinary	7 fantastic
3 everybody	12 exorbitant	9 extravagant	8 fantasy
2 everyone	10 exotic	6 extreme	1 far
2 everything	6 expand	6 extremely	9 farce
2 everywhere	9 expanse	9 extremity	5 fare
5 evidence	9 expansion	12 extricate	5 farewell
6 evident	13 expatiate	10 exuberant	1 farm
5 evil	12 expatriate	12 exude	2 farmer
12 evince	3 expect	11 exultation	2 farther
11 evoke	7 expectant	2 eye	6 fascinate
9 evolution	8 expectation	4 eyebrow	5 fashion
9 evolve	12 expedient	4 eyelash	P fast
13 exacerbate	5 expedition	4 eyelid	3 fasten
6 exact	7 expel		1 faster
3 exactly	9 expend		11 fastidious
7 exaggerate	9 expenditure	**F** 6 fable	2 fat
9 exalt	6 expense	7 fabric	6 fatal
4 examination	4 expensive	11 fabricate	9 fatality
4 examine	4 experience	5 fabulous	6 fate
3 example	4 experiment	2 face	P father
10 exasperate	4 expert	11 facet	7 fathom
7 exceed	13 expiate	12 facetious	6 fatigue
6 exceedingly	9 expire	8 facial	13 fatuous
8 excel	3 explain	13 facile	4 faucet
5 excellent	4 explanation	11 facilitate	3 fault
3 except	11 explicit	8 facilities	8 faulty
7 exception	4 explode	8 facility	4 favor
11 excerpt	10 exploit	12 facsimile	7 favorable
8 excess	6 exploration	4 fact	4 favorite
4 exchange	4 explore	11 faction	5 fawn
2 excite	5 explosion	13 factious	3 fear
3 excitement	6 explosive	7 factor	7 fearless
3 exciting	10 exponent		

10 feasible	3 fifty
3 feast	5 fig
6 feat	2 fight
2 feather	12 figment
6 feature	12 figuratively
3 February	4 figure
13 fecund	9 filament
3 fed	5 file
6 federal	13 filial
7 fee	2 fill
6 feeble	9 fillet
2 feed	6 film
2 feel	7 filter
1 feet	7 filth
10 feign	9 filtration
9 feint	4 fin
12 felicity	4 final
11 feline	10 finale
2 fell	3 finally
3 fellow	8 finance
9 felony	8 financial
2 felt	11 financier
5 female	1 find
7 feminine	1 fine
2 fence	12 finesse
6 fender	3 finger
9 ferment	2 finish
5 fern	13 finite
7 ferocious	5 fiord
10 ferret	6 fir
5 ferry	1 fire
5 fertile	1 fireman
5 fertilizer	4 firm
11 fervent	12 firmament
11 fervor	1 first
5 festival	12 fiscal
9 festive	1 fish
12 festoon	3 fisherman
6 fetch	11 fissure
12 fetid	4 fist
13 fetish	1 fit
11 fetter	1 five
7 feud	2 fix
9 feudal	12 fixation
5 fever	8 fixture
2 few	13 flaccid
8 fiancé	2 flag
8 fiancée	11 flagrant
12 fiasco	10 flail
5 fiber	9 flair
7 fickle	5 flake
7 fiction	3 flame
10 fictitious	10 flange
3 fiddle	9 flank
11 fidelity	8 flannel
8 fidget	3 flap
2 field	4 flare
7 fiend	2 flash
3 fierce	2 flashlight
4 fiery	7 flask
3 fifteen	3 flat
3 fifth	

——————— EDL Reading Core Vocabulary—Cumulative List ———————

7 flatter	10 folio	5 foster	5 frost	7 gamble	13 gesticulate
10 flaunt	4 folk	4 fought	10 froth	1 game	6 gesture
4 flavor	2 follow	6 foul	3 frown	12 gamut	P get
7 flaw	6 folly	1 found	5 froze	5 gander	7 geyser
9 flaw	4 fond	6 foundation	4 frozen	4 gang	4 ghost
6 flax	8 fondle	6 founder	10 frugal	6 gangplank	3 giant
6 flea	2 food	9 foundry	2 fruit	7 gangster	11 gibe
6 fled	3 fool	5 fountain	13 fruition	5 gap	3 gift
5 flee	3 foolish	1 four	10 frustrate	5 gape	6 gigantic
6 fleece	2 foot	3 fourteen	4 fry	3 garage	4 giggle
5 fleet	2 football	2 fourth	6 fudge	4 garbage	9 gild
5 flesh	P for	6 fowl	5 fuel	1 garden	8 gill
1 flew	11 forage	2 fox	6 fufill	7 gargle	8 gilt
8 flexible	12 foray	8 foyer	8 fugitive	12 garish	5 gin
4 flicker	11 forbearance	5 fraction	2 full	8 garlic	4 giraffe
9 flicker	6 forbid	13 fractious	6 fumble	5 garment	12 gird
4 flight	3 force	7 fracture	7 fumes	12 garner	8 girder
7 flimsy	6 ford	7 fragile	9 fumigate	12 garnish	1 girl
8 flinch	8 fore	7 fragment	P fun	9 garrison	10 girth
5 fling	9 foreboding	6 fragrant	8 function	13 garrulous	9 gist
4 flint	6 forecast	6 frail	7 fund	6 garter	1 give
5 flip	6 forefeit	3 frame	7 fundamental	3 gas	3 given
12 flippant	4 forehead	11 franchise	5 funeral	10 gaseous	13 glabrous
7 flirt	5 foreign	7 frank	6 funnel	5 gasoline	5 glacier
6 flit	6 foreman	7 frankfurter	P funny	4 gasp	1 glad
3 float	8 foremost	5 frantic	3 fur	2 gate	9 glamour
4 flock	13 forensic	9 fraternity	5 furious	3 gather	3 glance
5 floe	10 foreshorten	8 fraud	8 furlough	12 gauche	7 gland
4 flood	9 foresight	11 fraudulent	4 furnace	8 gaudy	4 glare
2 floor	3 forest	10 fraught	5 furnish	7 gauge	2 glass
5 flop	8 forestry	9 fray	4 furniture	7 gaunt	13 glaucous
8 floral	8 foretell	7 freak	5 furrow	11 gauntlet	10 glaze
13 florid	4 forever	4 freckle	4 further	5 gauze	4 gleam
7 florist	5 forge	3 free	6 furthermore	1 gave	10 glean
8 flounder	8 forgery	4 freedom	10 furtive	3 gay	5 glee
2 flour	3 forget	3 freeze	5 fury	3 gaze	10 glib
6 flourish	3 forgive	4 freight	6 fuse	5 gear	4 glide
3 flow	9 forgo	8 frenzy	8 fuselage	4 geese	5 glider
1 flower	3 forgot	6 frequent	12 fusion	6 gem	5 glimpse
5 flown	3 forgotten	3 fresh	4 fuss	10 gender	7 glint
11 fluctuate	4 fork	7 freshman	10 futile	4 general	4 glisten
8 flue	6 forlorn	6 fret	4 future	11 generalize	3 glitter
5 fluff	3 form	6 friction		5 generally	7 gloat
6 fluid	6 formal	3 Friday	**G**	5 generation	5 globe
5 flung	6 formation	1 friend		7 generator	4 gloomy
8 fluorescent	6 former	2 friendly	8 gadget	5 generous	9 glorify
6 flush	7 formerly	4 friendship	6 gag	8 genial	5 glorious
8 fluster	9 formidable	5 fright	9 gaiety	6 genius	5 glory
4 flute	7 formula	2 frighten	6 gaily	10 genteel	4 glossary
4 flutter	10 formulate	7 frigid	5 gain	3 gentle	6 glossy
13 flux	4 fort	8 frill	8 gait	4 gentleman	2 glove
1 fly	3 forth	6 fringe	10 gala	6 gently	4 glow
5 foam	8 fortify	6 frisky	9 galaxy	6 genuine	11 glower
10 focal	8 fortitude	10 frivolous	5 gale	5 geography	5 glue
7 focus	6 fortress	6 fro	6 gallant	7 geological	11 glut
6 foe	13 fortuitous	1 frog	5 galleon	7 geologist	10 glutton
3 fog	4 fortunate	8 frolic	6 gallery	7 geology	6 gnat
10 foible	3 fortune	1 from	6 galley	8 geometry	3 gnaw
7 foil	3 forty	2 front	4 gallon	6 geranium	P go
3 fold	10 forum	10 frontage	4 gallop	5 germ	5 goal
7 folder	3 forward	4 frontier	7 gallows	10 germinate	1 goat
7 foliage	8 fossil		8 galvanized		

———————— EDL Reading Core Vocabulary—Cumulative List ————————

4 gobble	3 grease	11 gusto	6 harsh	3 helping	10 hoax
5 goblin	2 great	6 gutter	4 harvest	6 hem	6 hobble
4 god	3 greedy	8 guttural	1 has	7 hemisphere	4 hobby
5 goddess	P green	6 guy	3 hasn't	1 hen	7 hobo
2 goes	4 greet	5 gym	7 haste	8 hence	5 hockey
6 goggles	12 gregarious	4 gypsy	6 hasten	1 her	5 hoe
1 going	2 grew		5 hasty	6 herald	4 hog
2 gold	5 griddle	**H**	1 hat	5 herb	5 hogan
4 golden	6 grief	4 habit	4 hatch	12 herbivorous	6 hoist
5 golf	9 grievance	11 habitable	6 hatchet	3 herd	1 hold
1 gone	6 grieve	11 habitat	3 hate	P here	7 holdup
7 gong	5 grim	8 habitation	7 hatred	8 hereditary	2 hole
P good	9 grimace	12 habituate	8 haughty	8 heredity	3 holiday
1 good-by	2 grin	12 hackneyed	5 haul	12 heresy	3 hollow
3 goodness	4 grind	1 had	5 haunt	12 heretic	5 holly
2 goose	4 grip	4 hadn't	13 hauteur	10 heritage	5 holy
10 gore	5 grit	8 haggard	P have	7 hermit	9 homage
5 gorge	6 grizzly	12 haggard	8 haven	3 hero	P home
6 gorgeous	4 groan	5 hail	2 haven't	8 heroic	6 homely
7 gorilla	4 groceries	2 hair	3 having	6 heroine	5 homestead
8 gospel	4 grocery	13 halcyon	10 havoc	5 heron	8 homicide
12 gossamer	6 groom	3 half	3 hawk	6 herring	13 homily
6 gossip	7 groove	3 hall	2 hay	2 herself	12 homogeneous
1 got	6 grope	12 hallowed	8 hazard	4 hesitate	13 homonym
4 gourd	7 gross	4 Halloween	5 haze	6 hesitation	4 honest
6 govern	10 grotesque	11 hallucination	6 hazel	12 heterogeneous	4 honesty
4 government	8 grotto	4 halt	P he	10 hew	1 honey
5 governor	1 ground	5 halter	1 head	13 hiatus	4 honk
5 gown	3 group	5 ham	6 headquarters	6 hibernate	3 honor
3 grab	6 grove	5 hamburger	5 heal	7 hiccup	6 honorable
5 grace	10 grovel	3 hammer	4 health	5 hickory	8 honorary
5 graceful	1 grow	5 hammock	3 healthy	3 hid	6 hood
6 gracious	3 growl	1 hand	4 heap	3 hidden	9 hoodwink
12 gradation	3 grown	6 handicap	1 hear	2 hide	3 hoof
4 grade	5 growth	4 handkerchief	1 heard	6 hideous	3 hook
4 gradually	6 grub	3 handle	7 hearse	13 hierarchy	3 hoop
6 graduate	7 grudge	4 handsome	3 heart	12 hieroglyphics	2 hop
6 graduation	9 gruesome	6 handy	4 hearth	1 high	2 hope
8 graft	5 gruff	3 hang	3 heat	3 highway	8 horde
3 grain	4 grumble	6 hangar	9 heathen	5 hike	5 horizon
5 grammar	4 grunt	6 hanger	7 heave	8 hilarious	7 horizontal
4 grand	7 guarantee	8 haphazard	3 heaven	1 hill	2 horn
2 grandfather	3 guard	10 hapless	2 heavy	8 hilt	6 hornet
2 grandmother	7 guardian	2 happen	8 hectic	1 him	10 horoscope
5 granite	10 guerrilla	3 happiness	6 hedge	2 himself	5 horrible
5 grant	1 guess	1 happy	6 heed	4 hind	6 horrid
10 granulate	4 guest	12 harangue	3 heel	6 hinder	4 horrify
4 grape	9 guidance	12 harass	13 hegemony	8 hinderance	5 horror
7 graph	3 guide	13 harbinger	7 heifer	4 hinge	1 horse
11 graphic	12 guile	3 harbor	5 height	6 hint	8 horsepower
4 grasp	6 guilty	1 hard	13 heinous	5 hip	10 horticulture
1 grass	5 guinea	2 hardly	7 heir	4 hire	3 hose
4 grateful	11 guise	5 hardship	7 heiress	1 his	8 hospitable
10 gratify	4 guitar	7 hardy	10 heirloom	5 hiss	3 hospital
12 gratis	6 gulf	5 hare	2 held	6 historical	6 host
5 gratitude	4 gull	3 harm	5 helicopter	3 history	8 hostage
13 gratuitous	11 gullible	6 harmonica	1 hello	13 histrionic	6 hostess
5 grave	6 gully	9 harmonize	6 helm	2 hit	7 hostile
5 gravel	5 gulp	7 harmony	5 helmet	4 hitch	1 hot
5 gravity	5 gum	3 harness	P help	3 hive	4 hotel
4 gravy	3 gun	5 harp	3 helper	8 hoard	3 hound
2 gray	5 gust	5 harpoon	4 helpful	4 hoarse	
4 graze					

EDL Reading Core Vocabulary—Cumulative List

3 hour
P house
6 household
10 hovel
5 hover
1 how
4 however
4 howl
7 hub
5 huddle
6 hue
3 hug
3 huge
11 hulk
5 hull
5 hum
4 human
7 humane
7 humanity
5 humble
10 humbug
10 humdrum
7 humid
7 humidity
10 humiliate
10 humility
5 humor
5 humorous
4 hump
3 hundred
3 hung
4 hunger
2 hungry
2 hunt
2 hunter
5 hurdle
5 hurl
4 hurricane
1 hurry
2 hurt
8 hurtle
3 husband
5 hush
4 husky
5 hustle
4 hut
10 hybrid
7 hydrant
10 hydraulic
6 hydrogen
5 hygiene
5 hymn
13 hyperbole
6 hyphen
7 hypnotize
10 hypocrite
11 hypothesis
10 hysteria

I

P I
1 ice
1 ice cream
5 iceberg
6 icicle
13 iconoclast
4 icy
3 I'd
2 idea
6 ideal
11 idealism
8 identical
8 identification
6 identify
8 identity
10 idiom
12 idiosyncrasy
6 idiot
5 idle
6 idol
11 idolatry
9 idolize
1 if
5 igloo
8 ignite
12 ignoble
12 ignominious
6 ignorance
6 ignorant
5 ignore
3 ill
2 I'll
8 illegal
9 illegible
10 illegitimate
12 illicit
9 illiterate
10 illogical
8 illuminate
9 illusion
7 illustrate
6 illustration
10 illustrious
2 I'm
6 image
11 imagery
5 imaginary
4 imagination
3 imagine
12 imbibe
13 imbroglio
12 imbue
4 imitate
6 imitation
11 immaculate
11 immaterial
10 immature
10 immeasurable
4 immediately
5 immense
8 immerse

6 immigrant
8 immigration
12 imminent
11 immobile
8 immortal
8 immortality
8 immune
13 immutable
6 imp
8 impact
8 impair
11 impale
8 impart
10 impartial
12 impasse
11 impassive
4 impatient
10 impeach
12 impeccable
12 impede
11 impediment
12 impel
11 impending
10 imperative
8 imperfect
10 imperial
11 imperil
13 imperious
10 impersonal
9 impersonate
10 impertinent
12 impervious
12 impetuous
12 impetus
13 impious
13 implacable
8 implement
11 implicate
13 implicit
8 implore
9 imply
6 impolite
5 import
6 importance
2 important
13 importunate
6 impose
3 impossible
9 imposter
12 impotent
10 impoverish
13 imprecate
10 impregnate
6 impress
6 impression
8 impressive
8 imprint
7 imprison
9 improbable
11 impromptu
8 improper
4 improve

4 improvement
13 improvident
7 improvise
9 impudent
6 impulse
9 impulsive
13 impunity
8 impurity
P in
8 inability
10 inaccessible
11 inadvertently
12 inalienable
11 inane
11 inanimate
8 inaugurate
11 inaugurate
9 inborn
10 incandescent
8 incapable
11 incapacitate
13 incarcerate
13 incarnate
11 incendiary
8 incense
8 incentive
12 incessant
3 inch
13 inchoate
12 incidence
6 incident
13 incipient
10 incision
10 incite
13 inclement
10 inclination
5 incline
5 include
10 inclusive
12 incognito
6 income
8 incompetent
7 incomplete
11 incongruous
8 inconvenience
10 incorporate
12 incorrigible
5 increase
7 incredible
11 incredulous
11 increment
10 incriminate
13 inculcate
12 incumbent
11 incur
9 incurable
9 indebted
3 indeed
12 indefatigable
8 indefinite
9 indelible
12 indemnity

6 indent
5 independence
6 independent
12 indeterminate
5 index
2 Indian
6 indicate
11 indict
8 indifferent
13 indigenous
13 indigent
7 indigestion
5 indignant
11 indignity
12 indiscretion
9 indispensable
10 indisposed
6 individual
12 indolent
12 indomitable
10 induce
10 inducement
8 indulge
7 industrious
6 industry
12 ineffectual
13 ineluctable
11 inept
10 inert
9 inertia
10 inevitable
13 inexorable
12 inexplicable
11 infallible
11 infamous
12 infamy
6 infant
8 infantile
9 infantry
10 infatuate
7 infect
12 infectious
11 infer
7 inferior
10 infernal
11 infest
10 infidel
11 infidelity
7 infinite
12 infinitesimal
9 infirmary
8 inflammable
8 inflate
9 inflation
11 inflection
8 inflict
6 influence
7 influential
7 influenza
11 influx
6 inform
7 informal

11 informant
4 information
12 infraction
11 infringe
8 infuriate
11 infuse
9 ingenious
12 ingenuous
12 ingratiate
7 ingredient
5 inhabitant
8 inhale
11 inherent
6 inherit
11 inhibition
13 inimical
12 inimitable
12 iniquity
6 initial
7 initiate
7 initiation
11 initiative
7 injection
6 injure
6 injury
4 ink
10 inkling
8 inlaid
8 inmate
3 inn
12 innate
4 inning
5 innocent
13 innocuous
11 innovation
12 innuendo
8 inoculate
12 inordinate
11 inquest
3 inquire
8 inquiry
11 inquisition
10 inquisitive
6 insane
12 insatiable
7 inscription
13 inscrutable
3 insect
11 insensible
11 inseparable
6 insert
2 inside
12 insidious
9 insight
9 insignia
9 insignificant
11 insinuate
12 insipid
4 insist
8 insolent
9 insomnia
13 insouciance

EDL Reading Core Vocabulary—Cumulative List

5 inspect
6 inspection
8 inspiration
6 inspire
6 install
8 installation
8 installment
4 instant
9 instantaneous
3 instead
11 instigate
8 instill
6 instinct
6 institute
7 institution
5 instruct
5 instruction
7 instructor
4 instrument
11 instrumental
10 insufferable
8 insulation
6 insult
13 insuperable
7 insurance
7 insure
13 insurgent
11 insurrection
9 intact
9 intangible
11 integral
8 integrate
9 integrity
7 intellectual
5 intelligence
5 intelligent
12 intelligentsia
13 intemperate
3 intend
6 intense
10 intensity
7 intensive
5 intent
7 intention
11 interaction
11 intercede
8 intercept
3 interest
3 interesting
6 interfere
13 interim
6 interior
11 interject
11 interloper
11 interlude
7 intermediate
12 interminable
8 intermission
11 intermittent
11 intern
8 internal
6 international

13 interpolate
5 interpret
11 interrogate
4 interrupt
8 intersection
11 intersperse
5 interval
11 intervene
6 interview
8 intimate
11 intimidate
1 into
10 intolerable
10 intolerant
11 intonation
8 intoxicate
13 intransigence
12 intrepid
8 intricate
8 intrigue
12 intrinsic
4 introduce
6 introduction
8 intrude
11 intrusion
10 intuition
12 inundate
13 inured
6 invade
6 invalid
12 invalidate
11 invaluable
11 invariably
8 invasion
13 invective
12 inveigle
4 invent
4 invention
5 inventor
8 inventory
11 inverse
8 invert
10 invertebrate
8 invest
6 investigate
7 investigation
8 investment
12 inveterate
13 invidious
10 invigorating
10 invincible
5 invisible
5 invitation
3 invite
11 invocation
11 invoice
10 invoke
6 involve
6 inward
5 iodine
13 irascible
10 ire

12 iridescent
8 irk
3 iron
10 irony
7 irregular
11 irrelevant
13 irreparable
11 irrepressible
9 irresistible
13 irrevocable
5 irrigate
5 irrigation
9 irritable
8 irritate
P is
3 island
7 isle
2 isn't
7 isolate
6 issue
9 isthmus
P it
6 italics
5 itch
6 item
9 itemize
13 itinerant
12 itinerary
2 its
2 it's
3 itself
2 I've
5 ivory
6 ivy

J

4 jacket
11 jaded
6 jagged
4 jail
4 jam
4 janitor
4 January
3 jar
10 jargon
8 jaunt
4 jaw
6 jay
7 jazz
4 jealous
6 jeans
4 jeep
7 jeer
3 jelly
11 jeopardize
3 jerk
6 jest
3 jet
7 jetty
3 jewel
5 jewelry
5 jiggle

7 jilt
4 jingle
3 job
11 jocular
13 jocund
5 jog
2 join
6 joint
2 joke
2 jolly
6 jolt
5 journal
3 journey
8 jovial
3 joy
4 Jr.
7 jubilant
3 judge
6 judgment
9 judicial
11 judicious
5 jug
3 juice
3 July
P jump
5 junction
12 juncture
3 June
4 jungle
5 junior
5 junk
11 jurisdiction
8 juror
6 jury
1 just
5 justice
8 justify
5 jut
8 juvenile
12 juxtaposition

K

3 kangaroo
4 kayak
6 keel
5 keen
2 keep
3 keeper
6 keg
6 kennel
2 kept
6 kerchief
5 kernel
5 kerosene
4 kettle
2 key
7 khaki
2 kick
4 kid
7 kidnap
2 kill
7 kiln

7 kin
2 kind
5 kindergarten
6 kindle
5 kindness
11 kindred
11 kinetic
2 king
4 kingdom
7 kink
3 kiss
5 kit
2 kitchen
2 kite
1 kitten
7 knapsack
7 knead
4 knee
5 kneel
5 knelt
2 knew
3 knife
3 knight
4 knit
4 knives
5 knob
2 knock
11 knoll
4 knot
1 know
4 knowledge
3 known
7 knuckle

L

6 label
5 labor
5 laboratory
7 laborer
10 laborious
11 labyrinth
6 lace
5 lack
13 laconic
7 lacquer
4 lad
2 ladder
7 laden
6 ladle
2 lady
6 lag
3 laid
5 lair
13 laity
2 lake
1 lamb
4 lame
9 lament
4 lamp
6 lance
2 land

4 landlord
9 landmark
7 landscape
4 lane
4 language
12 languid
12 languish
6 lanky
4 lantern
3 lap
7 lapel
8 lapse
12 larceny
6 lard
2 large
2 larger
6 lark
6 lash
13 lassitude
6 lasso
1 last
6 latch
2 late
12 latent
2 later
10 lateral
6 lather
6 latitude
7 latter
12 laudable
1 laugh
4 laughter
5 launch
6 laundry
6 laurel
5 lava
8 lavatory
7 lavender
9 lavish
3 law
4 lawn
5 lawyer
8 laxative
11 laxity
2 lay
6 layer
3 lazy
3 lead
6 leadership
3 leaf
8 leaflet
4 league
3 leak
3 lean
4 leap
3 learn
8 lease
5 leash
4 least
4 leather
2 leave
2 leaves

EDL Reading Core Vocabulary—Cumulative List

6 lecture	P like	2 lock	11 lustrous	6 manager	8 masterpiece
8 lecturer	6 lilac	4 locomotive	11 luxuriant	11 mandatory	13 masticate
3 led	8 lilt	4 lodge	6 luxury	4 mane	5 mat
4 ledge	5 lily	3 loft	7 lye	8 maneuver	8 match
8 ledger	5 limb	3 log	3 lying	7 mangle	2 mate
2 left	7 limber	8 logic	8 lynch	11 mania	4 material
2 leg	12 limbo	8 logical	8 lyrics	7 maniac	11 materialistic
10 legacy	4 lime	9 loiter		6 manicure	10 materialize
6 legal	5 limestone	3 lonely	**M**	11 manifest	10 maternal
11 legation	5 limit	4 lonesome	12 macabre	11 manifold	10 maternity
4 legend	9 limousine	1 long	8 macadam	10 manipulate	6 mathematics
7 legible	4 limp	12 longevity	6 macaroni	6 mankind	7 matinee
6 legion	11 limpid	7 longitude	13 machination	4 manner	13 matriculate
6 legislature	2 line	P look	2 machine	11 mannerism	8 matrimony
9 legislature	11 lineage	1 looked	5 machinery	4 manners	13 matrix
9 legitimate	10 linear	5 loom	3 mad	10 manor	8 matron
6 leisure	5 linen	6 loop	5 madam	6 mansion	3 matter
4 lemon	5 liner	3 loose	1 made	5 mantel	4 mattress
4 lemonade	7 linger	6 loosen	8 maestro	6 mantle	6 mature
5 lend	11 linguistic	7 loot	4 magazine	6 manual	13 maudlin
4 length	4 link	6 lope	2 magic	5 manufacture	10 maul
11 lenient	7 linoleum	13 loquacious	4 magician	6 manure	11 mausoleum
6 lens	5 lint	4 lord	9 magistrate	6 manuscript	12 maxim
5 lent	2 lion	9 lore	12 magnanimous	1 many	8 maximum
3 less	4 lip	3 lose	12 magnate	3 map	P may
8 lessen	5 liquid	5 loss	4 magnet	5 maple	2 maybe
3 lesson	10 liquidate	1 lost	6 magnificent	5 mar	3 mayor
6 lest	7 liquor	2 lot	5 magnify	11 marauder	8 maze
1 let	7 lisp	8 lotion	13 magniloquent	4 marble	P me
11 lethal	3 list	8 lottery	10 magnitude	3 march	3 meadow
12 lethargy	2 listen	2 loud	7 mahogany	4 mare	8 meager
1 let's	10 listless	8 lounge	4 maid	7 margin	3 meal
1 letter	4 lit	2 love	2 mail	12 marginal	2 mean
4 lettuce	11 literal	3 lovely	8 maim	6 marine	11 meander
7 levee	8 literary	2 low	3 main	10 marital	3 meant
4 level	6 literature	3 lower	10 mainstay	12 maritime	4 meanwhile
4 lever	12 lithe	5 loyal	6 maintain	3 mark	6 measles
12 levity	13 litigation	8 lubricant	8 maintenance	3 market	4 measure
6 levy	6 litter	7 lubricate	6 majestic	8 maroon	3 meat
11 lewd	P little	13 lucid	5 majesty	6 marriage	6 mechanic
10 liability	1 live	4 luck	6 major	4 married	6 mechanical
7 liable	8 livelihood	2 lucky	6 majority	3 marry	9 mechanism
11 liaison	3 lively	12 lucrative	P make	4 marsh	4 medal
6 liar	6 liver	12 ludicrous	8 makeshift	7 marshal	6 meddle
11 libel	9 livery	6 luggage	2 making	6 marshmallow	12 median
8 liberal	6 livestock	13 lugubrious	11 maladjustment	13 martinet	12 mediation
8 liberate	8 livid	6 lull	10 malady	8 martyr	6 medical
5 liberty	1 living	7 lullaby	5 male	5 marvel	4 medicine
5 librarian	5 lizard	3 lumber	13 malevolent	5 marvelous	9 medieval
2 library	5 llama	13 luminary	11 malice	5 mascot	10 mediocre
5 license	3 load	9 luminous	9 malicious	7 masculine	9 meditate
6 lichen	5 loaf	3 lump	11 malign	5 mash	6 medium
4 lick	5 loan	11 lunar	11 malignant	5 mask	10 medley
4 lid	8 loathe	8 lunatic	13 malinger	13 masochistic	5 meek
3 lie	5 loaves	1 lunch	11 malleable	8 mason	3 meet
13 lien	7 lobby	5 lung	7 mallet	8 masquerade	7 melancholy
12 lieu	11 lobbyist	5 lunge	4 mama	5 mass	13 mellifluous
7 lieutenant	7 lobster	5 lurch	7 mammal	8 massacre	6 mellow
2 life	6 local	7 lure	5 mammoth	8 massage	5 melody
3 lift	8 locality	12 lurid	1 man	7 massive	6 melon
1 light	4 locate	6 lurk	12 manacle	4 mast	3 melt
4 lightning	6 location	9 lust	3 manage	3 master	5 member

—————— EDL Reading Core Vocabulary—Cumulative List ——————

11 memento	7 mileage	5 Mister	2 moon	7 muscular	6 navigator
11 memoir	8 milestone	7 mistletoe	6 mooring	11 muse	4 navy
9 memorable	13 milieu	4 mistress	4 moose	4 museum	1 near
8 memorandum	12 militant	9 mistrust	12 moot	5 mush	3 neat
5 memorial	5 military	7 misty	4 mop	4 music	12 nebulous
6 memorize	8 militia	7 misunderstand	6 moral	5 musical	4 necessary
5 memory	1 milk	6 mite	8 morale	4 musician	10 necessitate
1 men	2 mill	13 mitigate	8 morality	4 musket	6 necessity
6 menace	13 millennium	6 mitt	10 morbid	6 muskrat	2 neck
13 ménage	4 million	4 mitten	1 more	1 must	3 necklace
9 menagerie	7 millionaire	3 mix	8 morgue	4 mustache	13 necromancy
5 mend	7 mimic	4 mixture	8 morality	6 mustard	2 need
13 mendacity	3 mind	3 moan	13 moribund	8 musty	3 needle
11 menial	3 mine	6 mob	1 morning	10 mutation	6 needy
6 mental	5 miner	7 mobile	11 morose	9 mute	13 nefarious
4 mention	5 mineral	8 mobilize	8 morsel	8 mutilate	8 negative
11 mentor	7 mingle	4 moccasin	6 mortal	7 mutiny	5 neglect
7 menu	6 miniature	6 mock	8 mortar	4 mutter	11 negligible
12 mercenary	8 minimum	8 mode	8 mortgage	6 mutton	10 negotiate
7 merchandise	5 mining	3 model	9 mortify	9 mutual	5 Negro
5 merchant	5 minister	7 moderate	7 mosaic	6 muzzle	2 neighbor
7 mercury	6 mink	4 modern	5 mosquito	P my	4 neighborhood
5 mercy	7 minnow	5 modest	4 moss	11 myriad	3 neither
7 mere	6 minor	7 modify	2 most	2 myself	13 nemesis
5 merely	7 minority	12 modular	5 moth	4 mysterious	7 neon
8 merge	4 minstrel	12 modulate	P mother	4 mystery	13 neophyte
7 merit	6 mint	6 moist	11 motif	10 mystical	4 nephew
12 meritorious	2 minute	6 moisture	4 motion	8 mystify	5 nerve
6 mermaid	5 miracle	8 molar	8 motive	4 myth	4 nervous
2 merry	7 miraculous	5 molasses	12 motley	8 mythology	13 nescience
4 mesa	7 mirage	5 mold	3 motor		1 nest
7 mesh	10 mire	5 mole	5 motto		6 nestle
5 mess	3 mirror	8 molecular	4 mound		3 net
3 message	7 mirth	8 molecule	3 mount	**N**	11 neurotic
4 messenger	13 misanthrope	8 molest	2 mountain	5 nag	11 neuter
1 met	13 miscegenation	13 mollify	6 mourn	2 nail	7 neutral
12 metabolism	8 miscellaneous	8 molten	2 mouse	10 naive	1 never
3 metal	3 mischief	3 moment	2 mouth	6 naked	1 new
12 metamorphosis	6 mischievous	9 momentary	2 move	1 name	4 news
6 meteor	10 misconception	11 momentous	6 movement	10 namesake	4 newspaper
7 meteorite	9 misconduct	10 momentum	4 movies	3 nap	1 next
6 meter	13 miscreant	7 monarch	6 mow	5 napkin	3 nibble
6 method	11 misdemeanor	8 monarchy	1 Mr.	10 narcotic	2 nice
12 meticulous	5 miser	8 monastery	1 Mrs.	10 narrate	6 nick
11 metropolis	5 miserable	3 Monday	1 much	7 narrative	3 nickel
11 mettle	7 misery	11 monetary	2 mud	6 narrator	5 nickname
3 mice	6 misfortune	1 money	5 muffle	3 narrow	5 niece
5 microphone	9 misguided	6 monitor	4 mug	7 nasal	6 nigh
7 microscope	8 mishap	5 monk	4 mule	9 nasal	1 night
7 microscopic	8 misjudge	1 monkey	8 multiple	11 natal	6 nightmare
6 mid	8 mislead	9 monogram	5 multiplication	3 nation	5 nimble
8 midday	12 misnomer	13 monolith	5 multiply	4 national	2 nine
2 middle	13 misogyny	10 monologue	8 multitude	11 nationalism	4 nineteen
7 midget	8 misplace	7 monopoly	4 mumble	9 nationality	3 ninety
4 midnight	1 miss	11 monotone	5 mumps	5 native	4 ninth
6 midst	1 Miss	7 monotonous	12 mundane	4 natural	7 nipple
11 mien	6 missile	5 monster	7 municipal	8 naturalize	6 nitrogen
2 might	5 mission	6 monstrous	13 munificent	4 nature	1 no
5 mighty	5 missionary	13 montage	8 munitions	4 naughty	5 noble
5 migrate	12 missive	3 month	7 mural	7 nausea	3 nobody
6 mild	4 mist	6 monument	7 murder	9 nautical	11 nocturnal
3 mile	3 mistake	4 mood	4 murmur	6 naval	3 nod
			5 muscle	9 navigable	
				6 navigation	

1 noise
8 nomad
12 nomenclature
11 nominal
8 nominate
8 nomination
8 nominee
10 nonchalant
11 noncommittal
12 nondescript
3 none
12 nonentity
11 nonexistent
4 nonsense
4 noon
7 noose
4 nor
6 normal
3 north
4 northern
1 nose
5 nostril
P not
7 notable
10 notary
11 notation
5 notch
3 note
9 noteworthy
1 nothing
3 notice
8 noticeable
6 notify
5 notion
12 notoriety
8 notorious
8 nourish
7 novel
7 novelty
3 November
12 novice
P now
13 noxious
6 nozzle
12 nuance
10 nucleus
7 nude
5 nudge
5 nugget
4 nuisance
11 nullify
5 numb
2 number
6 numeral
6 numerous
7 nun
12 nuptial
4 nurse
5 nursery
2 nut
11 nutrient
11 nutritious

12 nuture
6 nylon
8 nymph

O

2 oak
4 oar
4 oasis
6 oath
4 oatmeal
4 oats
13 obdurate
5 obedient
12 obesity
4 obey
10 obituary
4 object
6 objection
7 objective
7 obligation
5 oblige
10 oblique
11 obliterate
10 oblivion
8 oblong
10 obnoxious
10 obscene
9 obscure
12 obsequious
6 observation
8 observatory
5 observe
11 obsession
9 obsolete
7 obstacle
9 obstinate
8 obstruct
5 obtain
12 obtuse
12 obviate
6 obvious
5 occasion
6 occasional
11 occult
8 occupant
6 occupation
6 occupy
6 occur
8 occurrence
3 ocean
2 o'clock
4 October
5 octopus
5 odd
11 odious
6 odor
1 of
1 off
6 offend
6 offense
8 offensive

3 offer
2 office
4 officer
5 official
12 officiate
13 officious
3 often
1 oh
3 oil
8 ointment
1 old
5 old-fashioned
2 older
13 oligarchy
5 olive
7 omen
11 ominous
8 omit
8 omitted
12 omnibus
12 omnipotent
13 omniscient
12 omnivorous
P on
1 once
1 one
13 onerous
4 onion
2 only
11 onslaught
6 ooze
10 opaque
2 open
6 opera
5 operate
6 operation
5 operator
13 opiate
4 opinion
4 opossum
7 opponent
11 opportune
5 opportunity
5 oppose
4 opposite
6 opposition
8 oppress
8 oppression
13 opprobrious
8 optical
9 optimistic
7 option
12 opulent
1 or
6 oral
2 orange
8 orator
10 oratory
4 orbit
4 orchard
6 orchestra
7 orchid

9 ordain
8 ordeal
3 order
10 ordinance
4 ordinary
6 ore
3 organ
10 organic
10 organism
7 organization
6 organize
11 orgy
11 orient
11 orientation
12 orifice
6 origin
5 original
9 originate
4 ornament
7 ornamental
9 ornate
5 orphan
6 orphanage
12 orthodox
11 oscillate
13 ostensible
12 ostentatious
12 ostracize
6 ostrich
1 other
5 otherwise
3 ought
6 ounce
1 our
1 out
8 outcast
3 outdoors
5 outfit
8 outgrowth
7 outlet
6 outline
6 outrage
6 outrigger
2 outside
8 outskirts
6 outstanding
5 outwit
6 oval
2 oven
1 over
11 overbearing
6 overboard
8 overcast
7 overcome
7 overdue
8 overhaul
4 overhead
8 overlap
8 overlay
6 overlook
9 overpower
7 oversight

12 overt
6 overtake
10 overture
9 overwhelm
4 owe
2 owl
2 own
7 ownership
4 ox
5 oxen
5 oxygen
5 oyster

P

5 pace
11 pacifist
8 pacify
3 pack
3 package
8 pact
4 pad
4 paddle
8 pagan
3 page
6 pageant
3 paid
2 pail
4 pain
6 painful
1 paint
1 painted
1 painter
1 painting
2 pair
5 pajamas
5 pal
3 palace
11 palatable
3 pale
13 palliative
12 pallid
11 pallor
4 palm
13 palpable
11 palpitate
8 pamper
7 pamphlet
2 pan
12 panacea
13 pandemic
12 pandemonium
6 pane
13 panegyric
6 panel
5 panic
10 panorama
5 pansy
4 pant
5 panther
8 pantomime
5 pantry

4 pants
4 papa
2 paper
9 papoose
11 parable
4 parachute
1 parade
6 paradise
11 paradox
12 paragon
4 paragraph
5 parakeet
5 parallel
8 paralysis
7 paralyze
12 paraphernalia
12 paraphrase
9 parasite
6 parcel
7 parch
7 parchment
5 pardon
7 pare
3 parent
12 pariah
8 parish
1 park
5 parka
12 parlance
11 parley
6 parliament
5 parlor
10 parochial
12 parody
7 parole
13 paroxysm
4 parrot
10 parry
13 parsimonious
2 part
7 partial
7 participate
7 particle
4 particular
11 partisan
8 partition
4 partner
1 party
13 parvenu
2 pass
5 passage
10 passé
3 passenger
7 passion
10 passive
8 passport
2 past
3 paste
8 pastel
8 pasteurize
6 pastime
7 pastor

EDL Reading Core Vocabulary—Cumulative List

12 pastoral	6 peg	10 perseverance	5 pickle	5 plank	2 point
7 pastry	6 pelt	13 persiflage	1 picnic	3 planned	7 poise
4 pasture	3 pen	7 persist	10 pictorial	2 plant	4 poison
2 pat	11 penal	8 persistence	1 picture	5 plantation	5 poisonous
3 patch	8 penalize	4 person	7 picturesque	7 plaque	3 poke
7 patent	8 penalty	6 personal	2 pie	8 plasma	4 polar
10 paternal	12 penance	9 personal	2 piece	5 plaster	3 pole
3 path	13 penchant	6 personality	5 pier	6 plastic	13 polemic
8 pathetic	3 pencil	12 personify	5 pierce	3 plate	3 police
12 pathological	9 pending	11 personnel	8 piety	6 plateau	2 policeman
11 pathos	7 pendulum	10 perspective	1 pig	4 platform	7 policy
5 patience	7 penetentiary	13 perspicacious	4 pigeon	7 platinum	4 polish
4 patient	7 penetrate	6 perspiration	10 pigment	12 platitude	3 polite
5 patio	7 peninsula	4 persuade	2 pile	9 platoon	6 political
12 patriarch	12 penitent	8 pertain	9 pilfer	6 platter	8 politician
12 patrician	9 pennant	10 pertinent	4 pilgrim	12 plaudit	6 politics
6 patriot	2 pennies	8 perturb	10 pilgrimage	10 plausible	7 poll
6 patriotic	1 penny	11 peruse	5 pill	P play	8 pollen
6 patriotism	7 pension	12 pervade	11 pillage	4 playful	11 pollinate
5 patrol	10 pensive	12 perverse	4 pillar	4 playground	13 polyglot
10 patron	8 penthouse	10 pessimistic	3 pillow	4 playmate	8 pollute
11 patronage	13 penumbra	6 pest	3 pilot	6 plea	5 polo
10 patronize	13 penury	12 pestilence	3 pin	5 plead	11 polygamy
4 pattern	1 people	1 pet	4 pinch	3 pleasant	11 pompous
8 pauper	5 pep	7 petal	3 pine	1 please	5 poncho
4 pause	4 pepper	10 petite	5 pineapple	5 pleasure	2 pond
6 pave	6 per	8 petition	12 pinion	12 plebeian	6 ponder
6 pavement	9 perceive	6 petrify	2 pink	5 pledge	12 ponderous
2 paw	6 percent	5 petroleum	10 pinnacle	6 plentiful	1 pony
8 pawn	10 perception	5 petticoat	6 pint	3 plenty	3 pool
2 pay	5 perch	8 petty	4 pinto	13 plethora	2 poor
7 payment	13 peremptory	12 petulant	4 pioneer	10 pliable	2 pop
3 pea	11 perennial	6 pew	8 pious	6 pliers	2 popcorn
4 peace	4 perfect	9 pewter	2 pipe	8 plight	4 poppy
4 peaceful	8 perfection	6 phantom	12 piquant	5 plod	11 populace
4 peach	13 perfidious	8 pharmacy	12 pique	5 plot	4 popular
6 peacock	8 perforate	7 phase	4 pirate	3 plow	10 populate
5 peak	4 perform	6 pheasant	12 pirouette	5 pluck	5 population
6 peal	6 performance	10 phenomenal	5 pistol	4 plug	11 populous
1 peanut	5 perfume	7 phenomenon	8 piston	4 plum	6 porcelain
4 pear	12 perfunctory	7 philanthropist	4 pit	8 plumage	3 porch
4 pearl	3 perhaps	11 philanthropy	3 pitch	6 plumber	5 porcupine
5 peasant	5 peril	13 philistine	3 pitcher	5 plume	5 pore
5 pebble	8 perimeter	13 philology	10 piteous	12 plummet	6 pork
6 pecan	4 period	5 philosopher	8 pitfall	5 plump	9 porous
13 peccadillo	8 periodical	11 philosophy	7 pitiful	6 plunder	6 porridge
5 peck	13 peripatetic	12 phlegmatic	12 pittance	4 plunge	4 port
5 peculiar	7 periscope	4 phone	4 pity	6 plural	6 portable
13 pecuniary	5 perish	5 phonograph	8 pivot	12 plurality	10 portal
12 pedagogy	7 perishable	6 photograph	8 placard	6 plus	13 portend
4 pedal	11 perjury	6 photographer	13 placate	8 ply	4 porter
13 pedantic	6 permanent	8 photostat	2 place	7 plywood	8 portfolio
6 peddle	11 permeate	6 phrase	11 placid	5 P.M.	6 portion
3 peddler	4 permission	5 physical	12 plagiarize	12 pneumatic	10 portly
8 pedestal	5 permit	6 physician	7 plague	8 pneumonia	8 portrait
8 pedestrian	13 permutation	8 physicist	8 plaid	8 poach	8 portray
8 pedigree	13 pernicious	8 physics	3 plain	1 pocket	7 pose
3 peek	8 perpendicular	11 physiology	12 plaintive	5 pod	4 position
4 peel	11 perpetrate	9 physique	3 plan	5 poem	6 positive
2 peep	7 perpetual	3 piano	3 plane	6 poet	6 possess
5 peer	5 perplex	2 pick	4 planet	6 poetry	4 possession
11 peerless	7 persecute	5 picket	13 plangent	12 poignant	8 possibility

59

3 possible	6 prefer	8 prior	3 promise	8 provisional	2 push
4 possibly	7 preferable	9 priority	12 promissory	8 provoke	13 pusillanimous
3 post	7 preference	9 prism	12 promontory	6 prow	1 put
5 postage	9 prefix	4 prison	6 promote	12 prowess	10 putrid
5 poster	10 pregnant	4 prisoner	6 promotion	5 prowl	7 putty
11 posterior	9 prehistoric	13 pristine	5 prompt	12 proximity	3 puzzle
8 posterity	7 prejudice	8 privacy	13 promulgate	11 proxy	8 pygmy
12 posthumous	10 preliminary	4 private	8 prone	10 prudent	7 pyramid
4 postman	10 prelude	12 privation	7 prong	6 prune	
7 postpone	10 premature	6 privilege	4 pronounce	7 pry	**Q**
8 postscript	7 premium	1 prize	5 pronunciation	7 psalm	2 quack
12 postulate	11 premonition	8 probability	4 proof	12 pseudo	11 quadrant
6 posture	10 preoccupy	7 probable	5 prop	12 pseudonym	9 quadruple
3 pot	8 prepaid	3 probably	8 propaganda	12 psyche	12 quaff
3 potato	4 preparation	9 probation	12 propagate	10 psychiatrist	5 quail
11 potent	3 prepare	8 probe	7 propel	10 psychology	6 quaint
8 potential	11 preponderance	13 probity	9 propel	11 psychosis	8 quake
8 potion	11 preposterous	4 problem	5 propeller	5 public	7 qualification
4 pottery	12 prerogative	8 procedure	13 propensity	7 publication	6 qualify
5 pouch	13 prescience	5 proceed	5 proper	7 publicity	5 quality
6 poultry	8 prescribe	6 process	5 properly	6 publish	10 qualm
5 pounce	8 prescription	6 procession	4 property	6 publisher	10 quandary
3 pound	5 presence	6 proclaim	8 prophecy	5 pudding	6 quantity
3 pour	2 present	8 proclamation	8 prophet	2 puddle	5 quarantine
7 pout	12 presentiment	12 procrastinate	13 propiquity	13 puerile	4 quarrel
5 poverty	4 preserve	13 procreate	13 propitiate	3 puff	6 quarry
4 powder	7 preside	11 procure	12 propitious	11 pugilist	4 quart
3 power	3 president	11 prodigal	6 proportion	11 pugnacious	4 quarter
6 powerful	6 presidential	12 prodigious	7 proposal	1 pull	7 quartet
5 practical	3 press	12 prodigy	6 propose	5 pulley	3 queen
3 practice	5 pressure	5 produce	7 proposition	6 pulp	4 queer
12 pragmatic	7 prestige	5 product	12 propound	8 pulpit	10 quell
4 prairie	10 prestige	6 production	7 proprietor	6 pulse	7 quench
4 praise	6 presume	11 profane	11 propriety	10 pulverize	13 querulous
4 prance	11 presumptuous	10 profess	8 propulsion	4 pump	11 query
7 prank	3 pretend	6 profession	12 prosaic	4 pumpkin	7 quest
4 pray	8 pretense	6 professional	10 prose	5 punch	2 question
4 prayer	12 pretentious	4 professor	8 prosecute	13 punctilious	8 questionnaire
5 preach	12 pretext	10 proficient	6 prospect	7 punctual	11 quibble
11 precarious	1 pretty	8 profile	7 prospector	7 punctuate	2 quick
9 precaution	6 prevail	5 profit	11 prospectus	7 punctuation	2 quickly
7 precede	10 prevalent	6 profitable	8 prosper	7 puncture	12 quiescent
12 precedent	12 prevaricate	8 profound	8 prosperity	13 pundit	2 quiet
12 precept	5 prevent	11 profuse	8 prosperous	12 pungent	4 quill
10 precinct	6 prevention	13 progeny	11 prostrate	4 punish	4 quilt
4 precious	8 preview	4 program	13 protagonist	6 punishment	12 quintessence
8 precipice	6 previous	5 progress	4 protect	4 pup	4 quit
8 precipitation	5 prey	10 progression	4 protection	4 pupil	3 quite
8 precise	3 price	7 progressive	12 protégé	2 puppet	4 quiver
7 precision	4 prick	7 prohibit	4 protest	1 puppy	13 quixotic
12 preclude	4 pride	11 prohibition	12 protocol	5 purchase	6 quiz
12 precocious	6 priest	5 project	12 prototype	5 pure	8 quizzical
13 precursor	8 prim	11 projectile	12 protract	11 purge	8 quota
12 predatory	6 primary	9 projection	8 protrude	6 purify	6 quotation
12 predecessor	6 prime	8 projector	2 proud	8 purity	8 quote
8 predicament	11 primeval	12 proletariat	3 prove	3 purple	13 quotidian
7 predict	7 primitive	12 prolific	8 proverb	13 purport	
13 predilection	4 prince	13 prolix	5 provide	4 purpose	**R**
10 predominant	2 princess	8 prolong	10 providence	5 purse	6 rabbi
12 preeminent	5 principal	11 promenade	7 province	12 pursuant	1 rabbit
8 prefabricated	5 principle	7 prominent	10 provincial	7 pursue	11 rabble
9 preface	2 print	12 promiscuous	7 provision	7 pursuit	11 rabid

EDL Reading Core Vocabulary—Cumulative List

2 raccoon	11 raucous	8 recoil	12 regenerate	10 remittance	6 request
2 race	9 ravage	7 recollection	11 regent	7 remnant	6 require
8 racial	7 rave	6 recommend	9 regime	13 remonstrate	8 requirement
3 rack	5 raven	8 recommendation	11 regimen	8 remorse	11 requisite
4 racket	6 ravenous	12 recompense	5 regiment	6 remote	8 requisition
13 raconteur	10 ravenous	10 reconcile	5 region	8 removal	13 rescind
6 radar	5 ravine	13 recondite	6 register	4 remove	3 rescue
7 radiant	10 ravish	11 reconnaissance	8 registration	11 remuneration	6 research
10 radiate	5 raw	3 record	5 regret	11 renaissance	6 resemble
6 radiator	5 ray	8 recorder	8 regrettable	10 rend	6 resent
10 radical	7 rayon	12 recount	4 regular	7 render	4 reservation
2 radio	12 raze	11 recourse	6 regulation	8 renegade	6 reserve
6 radish	7 razor	6 recover	7 regulator	11 renegade	6 reservoir
8 radium	2 reach	8 recovery	12 regurgitate	7 renew	7 reside
7 radius	8 reaction	6 recreation	10 rehabilitate	8 renewal	7 residence
6 raft	1 read	12 recrimination	8 rehearsal	8 renounce	7 resident
7 rafter	6 readily	8 recruit	5 rehearse	10 renovate	7 residential
2 rag	8 readiness	7 rectangle	7 reign	9 renown	10 residue
4 rage	10 readjust	10 rectify	10 reimburse	4 rent	6 resign
4 ragged	1 ready	13 recumbent	4 reindeer	7 rental	12 resilient
5 raid	2 real	10 recuperate	8 reinforce	10 reorganize	6 resist
5 rail	11 realist	8 recur	4 reins	3 repair	6 resistance
2 railroad	8 reality	11 recurrence	10 reinstate	12 reparation	11 resolute
6 railway	4 realize	P red	12 reiterate	12 repartée	5 resolution
12 raiment	2 really	9 redeem	7 reject	5 repay	6 resolve
1 rain	7 realm	12 redress	5 rejoice	8 repeal	11 resonance
3 raise	6 reap	6 reduce	11 rejuvenate	3 repeat	6 resort
6 raisin	3 rear	8 reduction	8 relapse	8 repel	8 resource
4 rake	3 reason	11 redundant	6 relate	8 repent	8 resourceful
5 rally	5 reasonable	5 reed	6 relation	8 repertory	3 respect
5 ram	6 reassure	6 reef	6 relationship	8 repetition	8 respectable
11 ramification	11 rebate	7 reek	5 relative	6 replace	6 respectful
6 ramp	6 rebel	5 reel	5 relax	11 replenish	11 respective
11 rampant	7 rebellion	6 refer	6 relay	12 replete	7 respiration
6 rampart	9 rebound	6 referee	5 release	9 replica	12 respite
1 ran	10 rebuff	6 reference	12 relegate	3 replied	11 resplendent
2 ranch	7 rebuild	12 referendum	7 relent	3 reply	6 respond
12 rancor	13 recalcitrant	6 refine	12 relevant	4 report	6 response
9 random	7 recall	9 refinery	7 reliable	11 repose	6 responsibility
3 rang	13 recant	5 reflect	8 reliance	12 repository	4 responsible
4 range	12 recapitulate	5 reflection	8 relic	13 reprehensible	2 rest
6 rank	8 recede	8 reflex	4 relief	4 represent	5 restaurant
11 ransack	6 receipt	6 reform	6 relieve	7 representation	12 restitution
5 ransom	3 receive	10 reformatory	6 religion	6 representative	7 restless
8 rant	6 recent	12 refraction	6 religious	11 repress	11 restoration
6 rap	5 recently	13 refractory	11 relinquish	8 reprieve	6 restore
13 rapacious	8 receptacle	8 refrain	8 relish	9 reprimand	8 restrain
6 rapid	7 reception	9 refrain	7 reluctant	11 reprisal	8 restraint
3 rapidly	5 recess	8 refresh	5 rely	9 reproach	8 restrict
9 rapture	11 recession	5 refreshment	3 remain	12 reprobate	4 result
4 rare	6 recipe	4 refrigerator	7 remainder	8 reproduce	8 resume
8 rarity	12 recipient	5 refuge	5 remark	8 reproduction	12 resurgent
5 rascal	11 reciprocate	5 refugee	5 remarkable	11 reproof	11 resurrection
7 rash	7 recital	7 refund	9 remedial	9 reprove	8 retail
6 raspberry	7 recitation	6 refusal	6 remedy	6 reptile	8 retain
4 rat	6 recite	3 refuse	2 remember	6 republic	11 retaliate
6 rate	6 reckless	11 refute	7 remembrance	7 Republican	9 retard
3 rather	5 reckon	7 regain	4 remind	12 repudiate	11 retention
10 ratify	11 reclaim	9 regal	11 reminiscent	12 repugnant	12 reticence
8 ratio	8 recline	12 regale	12 remiss	9 repulsive	11 retina
6 ration	12 recluse	5 regard	13 remission	10 reputable	6 retire
10 rational	7 recognition	6 regardless	8 remit	5 reputation	6 retort
3 rattle	3 recognize				

EDL Reading Core Vocabulary—Cumulative List

9 retract	5 ripple	4 ruby
4 retreat	4 rise	5 rudder
11 retribution	13 risible	4 rude
9 retrieve	5 risk	12 rudiment
12 retrospect	11 rite	10 rue
2 return	10 ritual	6 ruffle
7 reveal	6 rival	4 rug
10 revel	7 rivalry	5 rugged
8 revelation	2 river	4 ruin
6 revenge	7 rivet	3 rule
8 revenue	7 roach	3 ruler
12 reverberation	1 road	4 rumble
8 reverence	4 roam	12 ruminate
8 reverend	2 roar	6 rummage
10 reverie	3 roast	6 rumor
6 reverse	4 rob	P run
10 revert	3 robber	5 rung
5 review	3 robe	1 running
13 revile	4 robin	10 rupture
8 revise	7 robot	6 rural
8 revision	9 robust	11 ruse
6 revive	2 rock	3 rush
10 revoke	4 rocket	5 rust
5 revolution	5 rod	8 rustic
5 revolutionary	2 rode	4 rustle
6 revolve	7 rodent	6 rut
6 revolver	4 rodeo	8 ruthless
10 revue	6 rogue	6 rye
11 revulsion	7 role	
3 reward	2 roll	
10 rhapsody	5 roller	
12 rhetoric	7 romance	
8 rheumatism	6 romantic	
5 rhyme	2 roof	
5 rhythm	1 room	
3 rib	7 roommate	
12 ribald	7 roost	
3 ribbon	3 rooster	
3 rice	3 root	
3 rich	2 rope	
11 ricochet	3 rose	
3 rid	10 roster	
4 riddle	10 rostrum	
P ride	6 rot	
4 ridge	6 rotary	
5 ridiculous	7 rotate	
2 riding	7 rotation	
13 rife	11 rote	
4 rifle	5 rotten	
10 rift	4 rough	
6 rig	2 round	
1 right	6 rouse	
9 righteous	8 rout	
6 rigid	3 route	
11 rigorous	7 routine	
4 rim	5 rove	
2 ring	9 rove	
5 rink	2 row	
5 rinse	4 royal	
7 riot	2 rub	
5 rip	3 rubber	
3 ripe	6 rubbish	

S

8 Sabbath	2 same	3 scatter
4 sack	5 sample	10 scavenger
6 sacred	12 sanctify	3 scene
5 sacrifice	11 sanction	4 scenery
12 sacrilege	8 sanctuary	7 scenic
2 sad	3 sand	3 scent
4 saddle	5 sandal	6 schedule
2 safe	3 sandwich	5 scheme
3 safely	7 sane	13 schism
3 safety	1 sang	5 scholar
6 sag	13 sanguine	1 school
8 saga	7 sanitarium	5 schooner
12 sagacity	7 sanitary	5 science
P said	8 sanitation	6 scientific
3 sail	9 sanity	4 scientist
3 sailor	3 sank	12 scintillating
5 saint	5 sap	12 scion
4 sake	5 sapling	4 scissors
13 salacious	9 sarcasm	7 scoff
4 salad	7 sardine	4 scold
5 salary	12 sardonic	4 scoop
3 sale	13 sartorial	4 scooter
12 salient	6 sash	10 scope
7 saliva	1 sat	8 scorch
10 sally	7 satchel	4 score
5 salmon	5 satellite	5 scorn
3 salt	13 satiate	8 scoundrel
13 salubrious	6 satin	7 scour
12 salutary	10 satire	11 scourge
4 salute	6 satisfaction	4 scout
7 salvage	7 satisfactory	4 scowl
8 salve	3 satisfy	4 scramble
	13 satrap	5 scrap
	10 saturate	5 scrape
	2 Saturday	3 scratch
	13 saturnine	3 scream
	4 sauce	4 screech
	6 saucer	4 screen
	11 saunter	5 screw
	4 sausage	6 scribble
	4 savage	10 scrimmage
	3 save	6 script
	3 saving	8 scripture
	11 savory	6 scroll
	1 saw	5 scrub
	2 say	11 scruple
	8 scaffold	10 scrutinize
	7 scald	5 scuffle
	4 scale	7 sculptor
	5 scalp	7 sculpture
	7 scaly	7 scum
	4 scamper	13 scurrilous
	6 scan	5 scurry
	8 scandal	4 scythe
	5 scant	2 sea
	11 scapegoat	4 seal
	5 scar	6 seam
	3 scarce	4 seaport
	3 scare	10 sear
	3 scarf	3 search
	5 scarlet	3 season
	12 scathing	2 seat

11 secede
10 secluded
2 second
6 secondary
7 secrecy
2 secret
5 secretary
9 secrete
8 sect
5 section
10 sector
12 secular
5 secure
8 security
7 sedan
11 sedate
11 sedative
12 sedentary
10 sediment
13 sedulous
P see
2 seed
5 seek
2 seem
2 seen
5 seep
5 seethe
10 segment
10 segregate
3 seize
5 seldom
5 select
6 selection
4 self
3 selfish
2 sell
11 semblance
5 semester
9 semicircle
6 senate
6 senator
2 send
12 senile
6 senior
6 sensation
3 sense
6 sensible
8 sensitive
11 sensory
11 sensual
2 sent
4 sentence
13 sententious
7 sentiment
7 sentimental
8 sentinel
6 sentry
5 separate
4 September
11 sequel
8 sequence
8 serenade

EDL Reading Core Vocabulary—Cumulative List

9 serene	4 sheriff	4 silence	6 slang	6 snack	3 somehow
5 sergeant	13 shibboleth	3 silent	4 slant	6 snail	2 someone
7 serial	5 shield	10 silhouette	3 slap	3 snake	4 somersault
5 series	4 shift	4 silk	5 slash	3 snap	P something
3 serious	6 shilling	4 sill	6 slate	5 snare	1 sometimes
6 sermon	5 shimmer	2 silly	6 slaughter	4 snarl	4 somewhat
5 serpent	3 shine	2 silver	5 slave	5 snatch	3 somewhere
7 serum	6 shingle	6 similar	6 slavery	4 sneak	12 somnambulist
4 servant	2 shiny	11 simile	6 slay	5 sneer	12 somnolent
3 serve	3 ship	3 simple	2 sled	4 sneeze	3 son
4 service	8 shirk	11 simulate	6 sledge	6 snicker	2 song
13 servile	3 shirt	10 simultaneous	6 sleek	4 sniff	13 sonorous
11 servitude	4 shiver	5 sin	1 sleep	7 snob	1 soon
6 session	5 shock	3 since	3 sleepy	6 snore	6 soot
2 set	1 shoe	5 sincere	6 sleet	4 snort	5 soothe
4 setting	1 shoes	5 sincerely	4 sleeve	6 snout	8 sophomore
4 settle	4 shone	13 sinecure	3 sleigh	1 snow	13 soporific
5 settlement	2 shook	5 sinew	4 slender	2 snowstorm	8 soprano
4 settler	3 shoot	1 sing	3 slept	9 snub	12 sordid
2 seven	2 shop	8 singe	5 slice	5 snug	4 sore
4 seventeen	3 shore	3 single	5 slick	1 so	10 sorority
4 seventh	2 short	8 singular	4 slid	4 soak	5 sorrow
3 seventy	8 shortage	8 sinister	3 slide	3 soap	2 sorry
9 sever	3 shot	4 sink	5 slight	4 soar	3 sort
3 several	2 should	12 sinuous	6 slim	5 sob	5 sought
11 severance	4 shoulder	5 sip	7 slime	5 sober	12 soujourn
5 severe	2 shout	8 siphon	6 sling	11 sobriety	5 soul
4 sew	4 shove	3 sir	3 slip	6 soccer	2 sound
7 sewer	2 shovel	7 sire	4 slipper	5 social	2 soup
7 sex	1 show	4 siren	4 slippery	11 socialist	4 sour
6 shabby	4 shower	2 sister	6 slit	5 society	6 source
5 shack	6 shred	1 sit	7 slogan	3 sock	3 south
3 shade	4 shreik	6 site	4 slope	6 socket	4 southern
3 shadow	7 shrewd	1 sitting	6 slot	5 sod	5 souvenir
5 shaft	5 shrill	5 situation	10 slothful	5 soda	7 sovereign
5 shaggy	6 shrimp	2 six	11 slovenly	10 sodden	6 sow
3 shake	7 shrine	3 sixteen	2 slow	5 sofa	3 space
2 shall	5 shrink	4 sixth	2 slowly	2 soft	5 spade
4 shallow	7 shrivel	3 sixty	9 sluggish	3 softly	5 spaghetti
9 sham	7 shroud	3 size	7 slum	5 soil	6 span
6 shame	5 shrub	2 skate	6 slumber	11 solace	6 spangle
6 shampoo	4 shrug	6 skeleton	6 slump	6 solar	6 spaniel
9 shank	5 shudder	10 skeptical	6 slung	3 sold	4 spank
3 shape	5 shuffle	5 sketch	9 slur	4 soldier	3 spare
3 share	8 shun	4 ski	6 slush	5 sole	3 spark
4 shark	2 shut	6 skid	5 sly	5 solemn	3 sparkle
3 sharp	6 shutter	4 skill	2 small	11 solicit	5 sparrow
6 shatter	3 shy	6 skillful	3 smart	12 solicitous	8 sparse
6 shave	3 sick	4 skim	6 smash	5 solid	10 spasm
4 shawl	5 sickness	3 skin	6 smear	13 soliloquy	3 speak
1 she	2 side	3 skip	2 smell	7 solitary	4 spear
5 shear	3 sidewalk	10 skirmish	10 smelt	10 solitude	3 special
7 sheath	7 siege	4 skirt	2 smile	6 solo	9 specialist
3 shed	9 siesta	6 skull	9 smite	12 solstice	6 species
2 sheep	8 sieve	4 skunk	9 smock	10 soluble	8 specific
6 sheer	7 sift	2 sky	3 smoke	6 solution	8 specification
3 sheet	3 sigh	8 skyscraper	3 smooth	4 solve	8 specify
3 shelf	4 sight	5 slab	9 smote	10 solvent	6 specimen
3 shell	2 sign	6 slack	5 smother	10 somber	13 specious
6 shellac	3 signal	6 slain	7 smoulder	5 sombrero	4 speck
4 shelter	6 signature	4 slam	7 smudge	1 some	4 spectacle
4 shepherd	8 signify	8 slander	6 smuggle	3 somebody	7 spectacular

—————— EDL Reading Core Vocabulary—Cumulative List ——————

7 spectator	6 spurt	2 station	6 storage	3 stump	2 suit
11 spectrum	5 sputter	5 stationary	1 store	5 stun	6 suitable
7 speculate	4 spy	5 stationery	2 stories	6 stung	4 suitcase
5 sped	7 squad	11 statistics	6 stork	5 stunt	7 suite
4 speech	6 squadron	4 statue	2 storm	10 stupefy	7 suitor
3 speed	12 squalid	12 stature	1 story	3 stupid	7 sulk
7 speedometer	11 squander	11 status	3 stout	10 stupor	7 sullen
4 spell	4 square	12 statute	4 stove	5 sturdy	12 sully
4 spelling	5 squash	9 staunch	6 stow	5 style	5 sulphur
3 spend	4 squat	1 stay	2 straight	10 suave	8 sultry
9 spendthrift	4 squawk	8 steadfast	4 strain	7 subdue	4 sum
4 spent	3 squeak	4 steadily	5 strait	5 subject	8 summary
7 sphere	4 squeal	4 steady	6 strand	12 subjugate	2 summer
5 spice	9 squeamish	5 steak	2 strange	13 sublimate	6 summit
3 spider	3 squeeze	3 steal	4 stranger	9 sublime	6 summon
4 spike	5 squint	9 stealthy	7 strangle	6 submarine	12 sumptuous
3 spill	5 squire	3 steam	4 strap	6 submerge	1 sun
3 spin	5 squirm	4 steel	10 strata	6 submit	3 Sunday
5 spinach	1 squirrel	3 steep	9 strategy	8 subordinate	10 sundry
4 spine	6 squirt	7 steeple	8 stratosphere	9 subordinate	4 sung
10 spinster	4 Sr.	3 steer	3 straw	7 subscribe	5 sunk
6 spiral	6 stab	3 stem	6 strawberry	7 subscription	13 superannuated
7 spire	10 stability	8 stench	3 stray	11 subsequent	8 superb
3 spirit	4 stable	7 stenographer	4 streak	12 subservient	12 supercilious
8 spiritual	4 stack	13 stentorian	3 stream	10 subside	9 superficial
6 spit	7 stadium	1 step	1 street	12 subsidiary	9 superfluous
5 spite	6 staff	11 stereotype	4 strength	12 subsidy	10 superimpose
2 splash	6 stag	10 sterile	8 strenuous	11 subsistence	5 superintenden
5 splendid	3 stage	7 sterilize	9 stress	6 substance	6 superior
8 splice	4 stagger	8 sterling	3 stretch	8 substantial	10 superlative
7 splint	10 stagnant	4 stern	10 strewn	6 substitute	9 supernatural
6 splinter	12 staid	5 stew	9 stricken	12 subterfuge	12 supersede
3 split	5 stain	6 steward	6 strict	8 subtle	6 superstition
3 spoil	2 stairs	2 stick	4 stride	5 subtract	10 superstructure
3 spoke	4 stake	3 stiff	13 strident	5 subtraction	7 supervise
6 sponge	6 stale	7 stifle	5 strife	7 suburb	7 supervisor
8 sponsor	4 stalk	10 stigma	3 strike	2 subway	13 supine
10 spontaneous	4 stall	2 still	2 string	4 succeed	2 supper
4 spool	4 stallion	11 stilt	13 stringent	4 success	12 supplant
3 spoon	10 stalwart	10 stimulate	3 strip	5 successful	11 supple
13 sporadic	8 stamina	11 stimulus	4 stripe	7 succession	9 supplement
4 sport	6 stammer	3 sting	8 strive	11 successor	12 supplication
7 sportsmanship	3 stamp	6 stingy	6 strode	13 succinct	4 supplies
3 spot	4 stampede	11 stint	4 stroke	13 succor	4 supply
9 spouse	10 stance	13 stipend	5 stroll	12 succulent	4 support
6 spout	2 stand	11 stipulate	2 strong	12 succumb	2 suppose
5 sprain	6 standard	3 stir	3 struck	2 such	9 suppress
4 sprang	8 stanza	5 stitch	6 structure	5 suck	6 supreme
5 sprawl	7 staple	5 stock	3 struggle	3 sudden	2 sure
3 spray	3 star	4 stockade	6 strung	2 suddenly	6 surf
3 spread	6 starboard	4 stocking	5 strut	7 sue	4 surface
1 spring	6 starch	12 stoic	5 stub	11 suede	13 surfeit
6 sprinkle	3 stare	4 stole	6 stubble	4 suffer	7 surge
6 sprint	11 stark	4 stolen	5 stubborn	9 suffice	8 surgeon
6 sprout	2 start	10 stolid	7 stucco	6 sufficient	8 surgery
6 spruce	3 startle	4 stomach	2 stuck	9 suffix	9 surly
6 sprung	7 starvation	2 stone	5 student	8 suffocate	11 surmise
7 spry	4 starve	2 stood	6 studio	12 suffused	11 surmount
5 spun	3 state	4 stool	9 studious	4 sugar	9 surpass
5 spur	4 statement	5 stoop	3 study	4 suggest	8 surplus
13 spurious	7 statesman	P stop	3 stuff	5 suggestion	1 surprise
9 spurn	8 static	1 stopped	4 stumble	7 suicide	4 surrender

EDL Reading Core Vocabulary—Cumulative List

12 surreptitious	11 synchronize	5 tawny	3 test	1 three	5 toboggan
4 surround	11 syndicate	5 tax	8 testament	7 thresh	2 today
12 surveillance	5 synonym	5 taxi	7 testify	2 threw	4 toe
5 survey	8 synopsis	4 tea	7 testimony	4 thrift	2 together
8 survival	11 synthesis	2 teach	7 tether	4 thrifty	5 toil
7 survive	10 synthetic	2 teacher	6 text	4 thrill	6 token
8 survivor	5 syrup	3 team	5 textile	5 thrilling	1 told
11 susceptible	5 system	4 tear	9 texture	5 thrive	10 tolerable
4 suspect	8 systematic	2 tease	1 than	3 throat	9 tolerate
6 suspend		6 technical	1 thank	5 throb	6 toll
7 suspenders	**T**	9 technique	4 thankful	4 throne	4 tomato
6 suspense	2 table	7 tedious	4 Thanksgiving	6 throttle	6 tomb
6 suspension	5 tablet	3 teeth	1 that	2 through	12 tome
7 suspicion	8 taboo	5 telegram	5 thatch	6 throughout	2 tomorrow
5 suspicious	10 tabulate	5 telegraph	5 thaw	2 throw	4 ton
7 sustain	13 tacit	2 telephone	P the	5 thrown	6 tone
12 sustenance	12 taciturn	4 telescope	5 theater	5 thrust	7 tongs
3 swallow	5 tack	9 telescope	6 thee	5 thud	4 tongue
3 swam	6 tackle	2 television	6 theft	4 thumb	7 tonic
4 swamp	8 tact	1 tell	1 their	4 thump	2 tonight
4 swan	2 tag	13 temerity	1 them	4 thunder	1 too
6 swap	1 tail	3 temper	6 theme	3 Thursday	1 took
4 swarm	4 tailor	10 temperance	3 themselves	5 thus	3 tool
9 swarthy	10 taint	8 temperate	1 then	9 thwart	2 toot
6 swat	1 take	4 temperature	10 theorem	6 thy	2 tooth
11 swathe	2 taken	7 tempest	5 theory	2 ticket	4 toothpaste
5 sway	4 tale	5 temple	11 therapeutic	5 tickle	2 top
6 swear	5 talent	9 tempo	1 there	4 tide	5 topic
5 sweat	1 talk	8 temporary	4 therefore	6 tidy	12 topography
4 sweater	2 tall	6 tempt	10 thermal	2 tie	5 torch
3 sweep	7 tallow	7 temptation	6 thermometer	10 tier	4 tore
3 sweet	7 talon	2 ten	5 thermostat	4 tiger	6 torment
4 swell	4 tame	12 tenacious	1 these	3 tight	5 torn
4 swept	4 tan	9 tenant	11 thesis	4 tile	6 tornado
8 swerve	10 tangent	5 tend	1 they	3 till	6 torpedo
3 swift	6 tangerine	8 tendency	3 thick	4 tilt	13 torpid
2 swim	9 tangible	3 tender	5 thicket	5 timber	7 torrent
8 swindle	4 tangle	8 tenement	3 thief	1 time	8 torrid
2 swing	3 tank	12 tenet	7 thigh	10 timely	10 torrid
5 swirl	10 tantalize	5 tennis	5 thimble	5 timid	10 torso
2 swish	12 tantamount	7 tenor	3 thin	13 timorous	5 tortillas
3 switch	9 tantrum	6 tense	1 thing	4 tin	12 tortuous
8 swivel	3 tap	9 tension	1 think	11 tincture	6 torture
6 swollen	4 tape	2 tent	2 third	5 tinder	3 toss
7 swoon	6 taper	6 tentacle	6 thirst	6 tingle	5 total
4 swoop	7 tapestry	11 tentative	3 thirsty	5 tinker	3 touch
4 sword	4 tar	4 tenth	3 thirteen	5 tinsel	4 touchdown
6 swore	4 target	11 tenure	3 thirty	6 tint	4 tough
6 sworn	7 tariff	4 tepee	P this	2 tiny	5 tour
4 swung	8 tarnish	11 tepid	6 thistle	3 tip	5 tourist
13 sycophant	6 tarpaulin	5 term	6 thong	11 tirade	5 tournament
4 syllable	10 tart	7 terminal	4 thorn	3 tire	5 tow
13 syllogism	5 task	9 terminate	6 thorough	2 tired	3 toward
12 sylvan	5 tassel	13 terpsichorean	1 those	6 tissue	4 towel
5 symbol	3 taste	5 terrace	6 thou	9 titanic	3 tower
10 symmetry	5 tatter	2 terrible	3 though	12 tithe	1 town
6 sympathetic	7 tattoo	5 terrific	2 thought	5 title	P toy
6 sympathy	3 taught	5 terrify	3 thousand	13 titular	5 trace
7 symphony	8 taunt	5 territory	5 thrash	P to	2 track
12 symposium	11 taut	4 terror	3 thread	4 toad	7 tract
7 symptom	6 tavern	11 terse	6 threat	3 toast	12 tractable
7 synagogue	10 tawdry	12 tertiary	4 threaten	5 tobacco	11 traction

EDL Reading Core Vocabulary—Cumulative List

2 tractor	5 trench	6 tuna	4 uneasy	3 vacation	6 venture
3 trade	13 trenchant	5 tundra	10 unerring	5 vaccination	13 veracity
7 tradition	8 trend	3 tune	6 unexpected	12 vacillate	8 veranda
3 traffic	12 trepidation	6 tunic	11 unfounded	5 vacuum	12 verdant
8 tragedy	6 trespass	3 tunnel	2 unhappy	6 vagabond	8 verdict
7 tragic	5 trestle	6 turban	4 unicorn	13 vagary	8 verge
3 trail	5 trial	7 turbulent	4 uniform	11 vagrant	9 verify
4 trailer	6 triangle	6 turf	10 unify	5 vague	12 veritable
1 train	3 tribe	13 turgid	6 union	5 vain	12 vernacular
7 trait	10 tributary	4 turkey	7 unique	4 valentine	13 vernal
5 traitor	6 tribute	9 turmoil	8 unison	8 valet	11 versatile
12 trajectory	1 trick	2 turn	4 unit	7 valiant	5 verse
4 tramp	5 trickle	4 turnip	7 unite	11 valid	7 version
6 trample	2 tried	7 turnpike	3 unite	9 valise	8 versus
8 trance	5 trifle	7 turpentine	3 United States	3 valley	10 vertebrate
11 tranquil	6 trigger	7 turret	8 universal	8 valor	6 vertical
9 transaction	4 trim	1 turtle	5 universe	5 valuable	13 vertiginous
12 transcend	7 trio	6 tusk	5 university	5 value	1 very
10 transcribe	2 trip	12 tutelage	10 unkempt	6 valve	5 vessel
4 transfer	7 triple	6 tutor	3 unless	6 van	6 vest
8 transform	9 tripod	4 twelfth	6 unravel	8 vandal	13 vested
10 transfusion	11 trite	2 twelve	7 unruly	11 vanguard	9 vestibule
11 transgress	5 triumph	3 twenty	2 until	6 vanilla	12 vestige
12 transient	6 triumphant	3 twice	13 untrammeled	4 vanish	7 veteran
8 transit	9 trivial	5 twig	3 unusual	5 vanity	9 veterinary
11 transition	6 trolley	5 twilight	12 unwitting	9 vanquish	8 veto
12 transitory	5 troop	1 twin	13 unwonted	11 vantage	7 via
6 translate	7 trophy	6 twine	P up	12 vapid	9 vial
11 translucent	4 tropical	9 twinge	12 upbraid	6 vapor	11 vibrant
8 transmission	6 tropics	4 twinkle	9 upheaval	10 variable	6 vibrate
8 transmit	3 trot	5 twirl	7 upheld	11 variance	6 vibration
13 transmute	2 trouble	4 twist	8 upholster	8 variation	12 vicarious
7 transom	5 trough	6 twitch	3 upon	13 variegated	6 vice
6 transparent	5 troupe	P two	8 uproar	6 variety	5 vice president
11 transpire	3 trousers	4 type	4 upset	5 various	6 vicinity
8 transplant	4 trout	4 typewriter	3 upstairs	6 varnish	5 vicious
5 transport	7 trowel	7 typhoon	5 upward	8 varsity	13 vicissitude
5 transportation	6 truant	6 typical	7 uranium	7 vary	5 victim
10 transpose	7 truce	11 typify	10 urban	13 vascular	7 victorious
3 trap	1 truck	6 tyrant	9 urchin	4 vase	4 victory
6 trapeze	13 truculent		4 urge	5 vast	11 vie
6 trash	4 trudge		6 urgent	7 vat	4 view
13 trauma	2 true	**U**	7 urn	7 vaudeville	10 vigil
13 travail	11 truism	13 ubiquitous	1 us	6 vault	10 vigilant
3 travel	8 trump	3 ugly	10 usage	13 vaunt	6 vigor
11 traverse	4 trumpet	11 ulterior	2 use	11 veer	7 vigorous
12 travesty	13 truncheon	10 ultimate	2 useful	3 vegetable	7 vile
4 tray	2 trunk	10 ultimatum	3 usual	6 vegetation	2 village
7 treacherous	3 trust	13 umbrage	3 usually	11 vehement	7 villain
6 tread	3 truth	4 umbrella	12 usurp	5 vehicle	12 vindicate
6 treason	1 try	4 umpire	13 usury	5 veil	12 vindictive
3 treasure	11 tryst	8 unanimous	6 utensil	6 vein	4 vine
4 treat	4 tub	1 uncle	12 utilitarian	8 velocity	5 vinegar
11 treatise	3 tube	10 uncouth	7 utilize	4 velvet	8 vineyard
6 treatment	7 tuberculosis	13 unction	7 utmost	9 vendor	11 vintage
4 treaty	4 tuck	13 unctuous	7 utter	8 veneer	8 violate
1 tree	4 Tuesday	1 under	13 uxorious	12 venerate	7 violence
6 trek	4 tug	5 underneath		8 vengeance	7 violent
3 tremble	8 tuition	3 understand		7 venison	5 violet
5 tremendous	5 tulip	3 understood **V**		7 venom	5 violin
8 tremor	3 tumble	5 undertake	8 vacancy	7 vent	13 virago
12 tremulous	10 tumult	9 undertone	6 vacant	8 ventilate	8 virgin
		13 undulate	9 vacate		

———— EDL Reading Core Vocabulary—Cumulative List ————

11 virile
10 virtual
8 virtue
11 virtuoso
13 virulence
6 virus
12 visage
7 vise
5 visible
5 vision
2 visit
3 visitor
8 visor
10 visualize
7 vital
10 vitality
7 vitamin
13 vitiate
13 vitriolic
11 vivacious
6 vivid
7 vocabulary
8 vocal
8 vocation
12 vociferous
11 vogue
2 voice
8 void
12 volatile
4 volcano
12 volition
5 volley
12 voluble
6 volume
12 voluminous
5 volunteer
12 voluptuous
7 vomit
13 voracious
5 vote
8 vouch
11 vouch
11 voucher
6 vow
6 vowel
4 voyage
7 vulcanize
7 vulgar
12 vulnerable
6 vulture

W
4 waddle
5 wade
6 waffle
2 wag
6 wages
1 wagon
10 waif
4 wail
4 waist
2 wait

6 waiter
11 waiver
3 wake
1 walk
1 walked
3 wall
6 wallet
6 walnut
4 walrus
6 waltz
10 wan
4 wand
3 wander
9 wane
P want
11 wanton
3 war
6 ward
7 warden
6 wardrobe
5 warehouse
5 wares
6 warily
2 warm
5 warmth
3 warn
7 warp
7 warrant
4 warrior
6 wart
7 wary
1 was
2 wash
2 wasn't
6 wasp
3 waste
2 watch
1 water
4 watermelon
2 wave
7 waver
5 wax
1 way
9 wayward
P we
3 weak
5 wealth
6 wealthy
9 wean
5 weapon
2 wear
4 weary
3 weather
4 weave
4 web
7 wed
5 wedding
5 wedge
4 Wednesday
4 wee
4 weed
2 week

3 weep
2 weigh
3 weight
6 weird
3 welcome
7 weld
7 welfare
2 well
2 we'll
7 welt
10 wend
1 went
6 wept
1 were
3 we're
3 weren't
3 west
4 western
6 westward
1 wet
3 we've
2 whale
4 wharf
P what
3 wheat
2 wheel
4 wheelbarrow
6 wheeze
1 when
1 where
10 whet
4 whether
2 which
2 while
7 whim
6 whimper
11 whimsical
4 whine
3 whip
4 whirl
5 whisk
4 whiskers
2 whisper
2 whistle
1 white
4 whittle
1 who
3 whole
8 wholly
4 whom
5 whoop
3 whose
1 why
4 wicked
2 wide
5 widow
5 width
8 wield
2 wife
4 wig
4 wiggle
4 wigwam

2 wild
4 wilderness
P will
3 willing
4 willow
7 wilt
8 wily
2 win
2 wind
1 window
5 windshield
4 wine
2 wing
3 wink
2 winter
3 wipe
3 wire
3 wisdom
2 wise
1 wish
9 wistful
5 wit
4 witch
P with
5 wither
9 withhold
1 without
5 witness
4 wizard
4 wobble
2 woke
2 wolf
1 woman
3 women
3 won
2 wonder
2 wonderful
6 wondrous
2 won't
2 wood
4 woodpecker
3 wool
1 word
3 wore
P work
2 world
3 worm
3 worn
3 worry
3 worse
5 worship
4 worst
3 worth
1 would
3 wouldn't
4 wound
5 woven
11 wrangle
3 wrap
6 wrath
12 wreak
5 wreath

3 wreck
6 wren
6 wrench
12 wrest
5 wrestle
7 wretched
6 wring
4 wrinkle
4 wrist
2 write
8 writhe
3 written
2 wrong
3 wrote

X
6 X-ray
13 xenophobia

Y
6 yacht
6 yam
1 yard
5 yarn
4 yawn
1 year
8 yearn
6 yeast
4 yell
1 yellow
5 yelp
P yes
4 yesterday
3 yet
6 yield
5 yoke
6 yolk
5 yonder
P you
2 you'll
2 young
6 youngster
1 your
3 you're
2 yourself
5 youth
3 you've

Z
8 zeal
13 zealot
12 zealous
11 zenith
4 zero
8 zest
6 zigzag
11 zodiac
4 zone
1 zoo

_____ **EDL Mathematics Core Vocabulary for Grades 1-3 and 4-6** _____

Math 1-3

A
abacus (III*)
about (III)
above (III)
across (V)
add (I)
addend (II)
addition (II)
addition sign (VII)
addition table (VI)
after (III)
algorithm (VII)
alike (VII)
all (in all) (II)
altogether (VI)
amount (III)
amount product (VII)
angle (III)
apart (VII)
Arabic numerals (VII)
area (III)
around (III)
array (VII)
as great as (VII)
as many as (V)
as much as (VI)
associative (VII)
associative law (VII)
associative property (VI)

B
base (VII)
base ten (VII)
before (III)
below (II)
between (III)
big (VII)
both (VI)
bottom (VII)
braces (VII)
by (II)

C
calendar (VII)
cardinal number (VI)
cent (I)
center (VI)
centimeter (IV)
change (IV)
changing the order (VII)
circle (III)
circular region (VII)
clock (III)
close (III)

collection (IV)
column (III)
combination (VII)
comma (VII)
common factor (VII)
common multiple (VII)
common property, -ties (VII)
commutative (VII)
commutative law (VII)
commutative property (VII)
compare (V)
compare, -paring sets (V)
complete (III)
complete the equation (V)
compute (VII)
concave (VI)
connect (V)
connecting points (VII)
contain (VII)
convex (VI)
coordinates (IV)
corner (IV)
corner point (VII)
cost (II)
count (III)
counting numbers (IV)
cube (V)
cubic (VII)
cup (III)
curve (III)
curved line (VII)
cylinder (VII)

D
day (II)
decimal (VII)
degree, -s (IV)
diagonal (VI)
diameter (VII)
difference (III)
different (III)
digit (III)
dime (III)
distance (V)
distributive (VI)
distributive property (VII)
divide (III)
dividend (VII)
divisible by (VII)
division (III)

divisor (VII)
do (V)
dollar (III)
double (V)
down (V)
dozen (III)

E
each (I)
edge (VI)
eight (III)
eighteen (VII)
eighth (VI)
eighty (V)
element (VII)
eleven (VI)
ellipse (VII)
empty (VII)
empty set (VII)
end point (III)
enough (VI)
equal (III)
equally (IV)
equation (I)
equilateral (VII)
equivalence (VII)
equivalent (IV)
equivalent sets (VI)
estimate (IV)
estimating area (VII)
even (III)
even number (III)
expand (VII)
expanded notation (V)
expanded numeral (VI)

F
fact (IV)
factor (III)
far (IV)
fast (VI)
few (IV)
fifteen (V)
fifth (IV)
fifty (IV)
figure (III)
first (III)
five (II)
foot, feet (II)
form (horizontal) (III)
forty (IV)
four (II)
fourteen (VI)
fourth (III)
fraction, fractional (III)
frame (III)

from (II)
function (IV)

G
gallon (III)
geometric (VII)
geometry (V)
given set (VII)
graph (IV)
great (III)
greater than (III)
grid (VI)
group (III)
grouping principle (VII)
grouping property (VII)
grouping rule (VII)

H
half, halves (III)
half-past (IV)
height (VII)
hexagon (VII)
high (VII)
horizontal line (VII)
hour (III)
how far (VII)
how few (VII)
how long (IV)
how many (I)
how much (II)
hundred (I)
hypotenuse (VII)

I
identify (VII)
identity element (VII)
inch (I)
inequalities (VI)
infinite set (VII)
inquiry (VII)
inside (III)
instead of (VII)
intersect (VI)
intersection of sets (VII)
inverse (VII)
inverse operation (VII)
isosceles (VII)

J
join (III)
join sets (VII)
joining and taking apart (VII)
joining equivalent sets (VII)

_____

*Roman numeral after each word refers to Frequency Category.

EDL Mathematics Core Vocabulary for Grades 1–3 and 4–6

L

large (III)
last (IV)
lattice (VII)
left (II)
length (III)
less (III)
less than (II)
line (II)
line segment (III)
linear measure (VII)
liquid measure (VII)
little (V)
location (VI)
long (III)
long way (VII)
longer than (VII)

M

many (III)
match (III)
matching one-to-one/one-to-one matching (V)
mathematics (VII)
measure, measurement (III)
member (of a set) (III)
metric (VII)
middle (VII)
midpoint (VII)
mile (III)
million (VII)
minuend (VII)
minus (VII)
minute (III)
missing (II)
missing factor (V)
model (VII)
model factor (VII)
model set (VII)
money (III)
more (II)
more than (III)
most (III)
multiple (III)
multiplication (II)
multiply (III)

N

name (I)
name factor (VII)
naming numeral (VII)
natural order of numbers (VII)
near (III)
negative number (VII)
next (III)
nickel (III)

nine (III)
nineteen (VII)
ninety (IV)
ninth (VI)
none (VII)
nonequivalent sets (VII)
nonmetric (VII)
not (III)
not equivalent (VII)
number (I)
number of addition (VII)
number of a set
number family (VII)
number line (III)
number object (VII)
number pair (IV)
number pattern (IV)
number ray (IV)
number sentence, -s (III)
number word (IV)
numeral (I)
numeration (VII)
numeration table (VII)

O

object (III)
odd (III)
odd number (III)
once (VII)
one (I)
one-fifth (VII)
one-fourth (IV)
one-half (III)
one less (VII)
one more (VII)
one-third (V)
one-to-many matching (VII)
one-to-one (VII)
one-to-one correspondence (VII)
only (VII)
open (VI)
open and closed figure (VII)
open and closed sentence (III)
operation (IV)
opposite (V)
order (III)
order of counting numbers (VII)
order of numbers (VII)
order principle (VII)

ordinal (VII)
ordinal concept (VII)
ordinal number (VII)
ounce (III)
outside (III)
over (III)

P

pair (III)
parallel (VII)
parallel lines (V)
parallelogram (VII)
parentheses (VI)
part (II)
partition (V)
path (IV)
pattern (III)
peck (VII)
penny (III)
pentagon (V)
perimeter (VII)
piece (IV)
pint (III)
place (III)
place holder (VII)
place value (IV)
plane (IV)
plus (III)
plus sign (VII)
point (II)
polygon (V)
position (VII)
pound (III)
prime number (V)
principle (VI)
problem (II)
problem solving (III)
product (II)
property (VI)

Q

quadrilateral (III)
quart (III)
quarter (III)
quotient (III)

R

radius (VII)
ray (III)
rearrange (VII)
rectangle (III)
rectangular region (VII)
region (IV)
regroup (V)
relate (IV)
related equations (VII)
related facts (VII)

related number sentences (VII)
relation (VII)
remainder (IV)
remove (VII)
rename (III)
repeat (VII)
repeated addition (VII)
replace (III)
replacement (set) (VII)
represent (VII)
result (VII)
rhombus (VII)
right (III)
right angle (IV)
Roman numeral (V)
round (IV)
row (III)

S

same (III)
same as (IV)
same length (V)
same number (III)
same size (IV)
score (IV)
second (III)
segment (III)
sentence (I)
separate (IV)
separating sets (VII)
sequence (VII)
sequence of numbers (VII)
set (I)
set of points (VII)
seven (III)
seventeen (VII)
seventh (V)
seventy (IV)
shade (V)
shape (III)
short (IV)
short form (V)
short way (VII)
shorter than (VII)
side (III)
sign (III)
sign of relation (VII)
simple (III)
single (VII)
six (II)
six-sevenths (VII)
sixteen (VI)
sixth (IV)
sixty (V)
size (IV)

_____ **EDL Mathematics Core Vocabulary for Grades 1–3 and 4–6** _____

small (IV)
solution (IV)
solve (II)
solving (the) equation,
   -s (VI)
some (IV)
space (III)
sphere (VII)
square (III)
square unit (VII)
standard numeral (VI)
straight line (VII)
subset (III)
subtract (II)
subtraction (II)
subtraction pattern
   (VII)
subtrahend (VII)
such that (VII)
sum (I)
surface (VII)
symbol (IV)
symmetrical (VII)
symmetry (VI)

T table (III)
take-away (VI)
tall (IV)
temperature (III)
ten (I)
tenth (V)
thermometer (IV)
third (III)
thirteen (VII)
thirty (IV)
thousand (II)
three (I)
three-fourths (VI)
time (of day) (III)
times (III)
tiny (VII)
ton (VII)
top (VI)
total (VI)
triangle (III)
triangular region (VII)
triangular shape (VII)
twelve (IV)
twenty (III)
twice (V)
two (I)
two-thirds (VII)

U under (V)
undo (IV)
unequal (VII)

union (IV)
unit (III)
unit of measure (V)
unit of time (VII)
unit line segment (VII)
unknown (VII)
unnamed (VI)
unnamed factor (VII)
unnamed quotient
   (VII)
up (V)

V value (IV)
vertex, -tices (VII)
vertical (VII)
vertical form (VI)
vertical line (VII)
volume (VII)

W week (III)
weight (III)
which (V)
whole (III)
whole number (III)
width (IV)
word name (VII)

Y yard (III)

Z zero (III)

Math 4-6

A abscissa (IX)
acre (VII)
acre-foot (feet) (IX)
actual (VI)
acute angle (VII)
acute triangle (IX)
addition numeral
   (VIII)
additive (IX)
additive inverse (IX)
adjacent (IX)
align (IX)
alternate interior angle
   (IX)
altitude (of a figure)
   (VII)
angle bisector (IX)
angle unit (IX)
annex (IX)
approximate, -d, -ly (V)
approximately equal
   (equivalent) to (IX)

approximation (VII)
arc (V)
area measure, -ment
   (VII)
arithmetic, -al (VII)
arithmetic mean (VIII)
arithmetic sequence
   (IX)
associative operation
   (IX)
average (I)
avoirdupois system
   (IX)
axes (IX)
axis (VII)

B baker's dozen (IX)
bar (VII)
bar graph (V)
base (of a figure) (VI)
base eight (VII)
base five (IV)
base four (VII)
base number (VIII)
base numeral (IX)
base seven (IX)
base six (VII)
base ten machine (IX)
base three (VIII)
base two (IX)
basic facts (VII)
billion (V)
billions' period (IX)
binary numeral (IX)
binary operation (IX)
binary system (IX)
bisect (VII)
bisect an angle (VIII)
bisect a line segment
   (IX)
bisector (IX)
bound (IX)
boundary (VIII)
bracket (IX)
break (broken) apart
   (IX)
broken-line graph
   (VIII)
bushel (VIII)

C calculate, -lation (IX)
capacity (VIII)
carat (IX)
cardinal (*not* "cardinal
   number") (VIII)
caret (IX)

cast out (IX)
centigrade (VII)
centigram (IX)
centiliter (IX)
central angle (VI)
century (VIII)
cheap, -er, -est (IX)
chord (VI)
circle graph (VII)
circular cylinder (IX)
circumference (IV)
circumscribed (IX)
clock arithmetic (VII)
clock equation (VII)
closed (no other form)
   (VI)
closed curve (VIII)
closed figure (VII)
closed plane figure
   (VIII)
closed sentence (VI)
closed space figure
   (VIII)
closed surface (VII)
closure property of
   addition for whole
   numbers (IX)
closure property of
   division for whole
   numbers (IX)
closure property of
   multiplication for
   whole numbers (IX)
closure property of
   subtraction for
   whole numbers (IX)
code, -d, coding (V)
collected (no other
   form) (VII)
collinear (VIII)
column algorism form
   (IX)
combine, -d, -bining
   (VII)
commission (VII)
common (in common)
   (III)
common denominator
   method (VIII)
common factor
   property (IX)
commutative operation
   (IX)
commutativity (IX)
commute, -d, -muting
   (VIII)

compact numeral (VI)
comparison (VIII)
compass (IV)
complete factorization (IX)
completely factored (IX)
complex fraction (IX)
complex fractional numeral (IX)
composite (VIII)
composite number (VII)
composite sentence (IX)
computation (VI)
concentric (circle) (VIII)
conclusion (IX)
cone (geometric shape) (VI)
congruent (I)
connective (IX)
consecutive (VIII)
constant (IX)
construct, -ion (IV)
convert (VIII)
coordinate axes (IX)
coordinate axis (IX)
coordinate geometry (IX)
coordinate system (IX)
copy (-ing) an (the) angle (IX)
copy (-ing) a (the) (line) segment (VIII)
copy (-ing) a (the) triangle (IX)
cord (IX)
correspond, -ed, -ing (XI)
corresponding angles (VIII)
corresponding sides (IX)
counting man (men) (IX)
couple (IX)
crease, -d, creasing (VIII)
cross, -ed, -ing (VI)
cross-product (VII)
cross-section (IX)
cryptogram (IX)
cube root (IX)

cubed (no other form) (IX)
cubic centimeter (VII)
cubic foot (feet) (V)
cubic inch (VI)
cubic kilometer (IX)
cubic meter (IX)
cubic mile (IX)
cubic millimeter (VIII)
cubic (cube) unit (VI)
cubic yard (VI)
cubit (IX)
currency (IX)
currency breakdown table (IX)

D data (IV)
decade (VIII)
decagram (IX)
decameter (IX)
decigram (IX)
deciliter (IX)
decillion (IX)
decimal equivalent (IX)
decimal form (VI)
decimal fraction (VII)
decimal name (VIII)
decimal number (IX)
decimal numeral (IV)
decimal numeration (system) (VIII)
decimal place (VII)
decimal point (IV)
decimal system (VIII)
decimeter (VI)
decrease (VIII)
degree measure (VI)
dekagram (IX)
dekaliter (IX)
dekameter (IX)
denominator (I)
denote, -d, -noting (VIII)
density (IX)
deposit (VII)
depth (VII)
derive (IX)
determine (VIII)
diagram (IV)
dimension (VI)
discount, -ed, -ing (VI)
disjoint (set) (VII)
distribute (-d) over (VI)
distribution (IX)

distributive law (principle) for rational numbers (IX)
distributive law (property) for (of) division (over addition) (VII)
distributive law (property) for (of) multiplication (over addition) (VI)
distributive law (property) for (of) multiplication (over subtraction) (IX)
divisibility (VII)
division form (VIII)
division numeral (VII)
dodecahedron (IX)
dot graph (VIII)
double-bar graph (IX)
dry measure (IX)
duplicate (IX)

E Egyptian numerals (VII)
Egyptian (numeration) system (VIII)
end (VII)
English system (of measures) (IX)
equal sets (IX)
equality (sentence) (VII)
equality (equal) sign (symbol) (VIII)
equally likely (VIII)
equiangular triangle (IX)
equilateral triangle (VII)
equivalent decimals (VII)
equivalent equations (VII)
equivalent fractional numerals (V)
equivalent fractions (IV)
equivalent inequalities (IX)
equivalent measures, measurements (VIII)
equivalent numbers (IX)

equivalent numerals (VII)
equivalent ratios (IX)
error of measurement (IX)
estimation (no other form) (VII)
event (IX)
exact, -ly (IV)
expanded form (IX)
expanded fraction (IX)
experiment (number, problem) (VII)
exponent (VI)
exponential (exponent) form (VIII)
express, -ed, -ing, -ion (I)
extend, -ed, -ing (VI)
exterior (VII)

F face (IV)
face value (IX)
factor set (VII)
factor tree (VI)
factored form (IX)
factorial (IX)
factorization (IX)
Fahrenheit (VII)
family of facts (VIII)
farther, -est (VI)
fathom (IX)
finite (set) (VII)
first axis (IX)
first partial product (VIII)
first power (IX)
first term (IX)
fixed (VIII)
flat (surface) (VII)
fluid ounce (VIII)
foci (IX)
foot-pound (IX)
formula (V)
fortnight (IX)
fourth partial product (IX)
fraction bar (IX)
fraction line (IX)
fractional form (VI)
fractional name (VIII)
fractional number (I)
fractional number ray (IX)
fractional numeral (IV)
frequency (VIII)

———————— **EDL Mathematics Core Vocabulary for Grades 1–3 and 4–6** ————————

frequency distribution
(IX)
frequency table (IX)
full (VIII)
function equation
(VIII)
function machine (VII)
function rule (IV)
function table (IX)
furlong (IX)
f(x)-axis (IX)

G generalization (VIII)
geometric figure (VI)
given (V)
graduated (measuring)
scale (IX)
gram (VII)
graph of the (an)
equation (IX)
great circle (IX)
greatest common factor
(IV)
greatest possible error
(of measurement)
(VIII)
greatest possible
multiple (IX)
gross (IX)
gross weight (IX)
grouping symbol (VIII)
guess (VIII)

H half-circle (IX)
half-dollar (VII)
half-line (IX)
half-plane (VIII)
halfway (VII)
halved (no other form)
(IX)
hand (as in measure)
(IX)
hectogram (IX)
hectoliter (IX)
hectometer (IX)
helping marks (figures,
numerals) (IX)
hemisphere (IX)
heptagon (IX)
hexagonal prism (IX)
hexagonal pyramid
(IX)
hexahedron (IX)
higher terms (VIII)
Hindu-Arabic (VII)

Hindu-Arabic
(numeration) system
(VIII)
histogram (VIII)
holds a (the) place (IX)
horizontal (VII)
horizontal axis (IX)
horizontal bar graph
(IX)
horizontal coordinate
(IX)
horizontal scale (VIII)
hundred million (VIII)
hundred thousand (V)
hundred thousandths
(IX)
hundreds' digit (VIII)
hundreds' man (men)
(IX)
hundreds' place (VII)
hundredth (II)
hundredths' place (IX)
hundredweight (IX)

I icosahedron (IX)
identity element
(number) for (of)
addition (VIII)
identity element
(number) for (of)
division (IX)
identity element
(number) for (of)
multiplication (VII)
identity element
(number) for (of)
subtraction (IX)
identity property (IX)
if-then-not rule
(sentence,
statement) (IX)
if-then rule (sentence,
statement) (VIII)
imply, -plies (IX)
improper fraction (VII)
include, -d, -cluding
(VII)
inclusion (IX)
inclusive (VIII)
increase (VI)
indent (IX)
inequality sentence
(VIII)
inequality sign
(symbol) (IX)
inference (VIII)

infinite (VII)
input (VIII)
input number (VIII)
input-output card (IX)
inscribed (VIII)
insert (IX)
inspection (IX)
integer (IV)
interest (bank) (VII)
interest rate (VIII)
interior (IV)
(international) nautical
mile (IX)
interpret, -ation (VIII)
intersecting lines (VII)
intersection set (IX)
interval (VII)
isosceles right triangle
(IX)
isosceles triangle (VII)

K key number (IX)
kilogram (VIII)
kiloliter (IX)
kilometer (VI)

L landing point (VIII)
lateral area (IX)
lattice method (VIII)
lattice multiplication
(IX)
layer (VI)
leap year (IX)
least (IV)
least common
denominator (V)
least common factor
(IX)
least common multiple
(IV)
leg (of a triangle) (VII)
light, -er, -est (weight
only) (IX)
lightning multiplication
(IX)
light year (IX)
line of symmetry
(VIII)
line graph (VI)
line segment graph
(IX)
linear (IX)
linear pair (VII)
liquid (VII)
liquid measure (VIII)
liter (VIII)

locate, -d, -cating (VI)
long form (VIII)
long vertical form
(VIII)
loss (IX)
lower bound (VIII)
lower limit (IX)
lower terms (VIII)
lowest terms (V)
lowest terms fraction
(VI)

M magic number (IX)
magic square (VII)
major arc (IX)
marked up (IX)
markup (IX)
matching sides (IX)
mathematical phrase
(IX)
mathematical sentence
(statement) (VI)
maximal (IX)
maximum (IX)
mean (term for
average) (VII)
median (VI)
megameter (IX)
memory man (men)
(IX)
meter stick (IX)
metric geometry (IX)
metric system (VI)
metric unit (VIII)
micrometer caliper (IX)
micron (IX)
midway (IX)
miles per hour (IV)
millenium (IX)
milligram (IX)
milliliter (IX)
millimeter (VI)
millions' period (IX)
millions' place (IX)
millionths (VIII)
millisecond (IX)
minimum (IX)
minor arc (VIII)
mixed decimal
(numeral) (IX)
mixed numeral (III)
mixed-numeral form
(IX)
mode (VI)
month (IV)

multiples (of powers) of ten (VII)
multiplicand (IX)
miltiplication numeral (VII)
multiplication-addition principle (IX)
multiplier (IX)

N name line (IX)
natural number (VI)
negative (VI)
negative integer (VIII)
noncollinear (IX)
nondisjoint (VIII)
nonequivalent (IX)
nonillion (IX)
nonmetric (IX)
nonrepeating (IX)
nonstandard (IX)
nonstandard unit (IX)
nonterminating (IX)
nonzero (IX)
not prime (VIII)
notation (VII)
number of (the) set (IX)
number-naming board (VIII)
number plane (VI)
numeral-reading chart (IX)
numeration system (system of numeration) (VI)
numerator (II)

O obtuse angle (VII)
obtuse isosceles triangle (IX)
obtuse scalene triangle (IX)
obtuse triangle (IX)
octagon (VIII)
octahedron (IX)
octillion (IX)
one-hundredth (IX)
one-tenth (IX)
one-thousandth (IX)
ones' digit (VII)
ones' man (men) (VIII)
ones' period (VIII)
ones' place (column) (V)
open equation (IX)
open figure (IX)

open sentence (I)
opposite integers (IX)
opposite operations (IX)
ordered (number) pairs (IV)
ordered set (IX)
origin (IX)
original (VII)
original number (IX)
outcome (VI)
output (VII)
output number (VI)

P parallel planes (IX)
partial product (VII)
partial quotient (VI)
partial sum (IX)
pentagonal pyramid (IX)
per (I)
percent, -age (I)
percent equivalents (IX)
percent form (VII)
percent sign (symbol) (IX)
perfect (in terms of a number) (IX)
period (VI)
perpendicular (VI)
perpendicular bisector (IX)
perpendicular lines (VIII)
pi (Greek letter) (IX)
pictograph (VIII)
picture graph (VI)
place-value chart (VI)
place-value grid (VIII)
place-value numeral (VIII)
plane figure (VII)
plane region (VIII)
plot (IX)
polygonal region (IX)
polyhedron, *pl.* -dra (IX)
positional (IX)
positive (VII)
positive integer (VII)
positive number (IX)
power (VI)
power(s) of ten (VI)
precise (VII)
precision (VII)

predict, -ion (VIII)
prime (IV)
prime factor (V)
prime factorization (VI)
principal (interest term) (IX)
prism (VII)
probability (IV)
procedure (VIII)
product method (IX)
product numeral (VIII)
product of prime factors (VII)
product of prime numbers (IX)
product set (IX)
profit (VII)
progression (IX)
proper fraction (IX)
proportion (VI)
protractor (VI)
pyramid (VII)
Pythagoras' (Pythagorean) theorem (IX)

Q quadrillion (IX)
quantity (IX)
quarter inch (VIII)
quintillion (IX)
quire (IX)
quotient numeral (VII)

R radian (IX)
radii (VII)
range of measurement
range (of scores) (VI)
ranking list (IX)
rate (IV)
rate of commission (VIII)
rate of discount (VIII)
rate of interest (IX)
rate of speed (travel) (IX)
ratio (I)
ratio form (IX)
ratio interpretation of multiplication (IX)
rational number (I)
reciprocal (V)
rectangular prism (V)
rectangular pyramid (IX)
rectangular solid (VII)

reduce, -d, -ducing (VII)
reduction (IX)
reference line (IX)
reflexive property (IX)
regular (VI)
regular polygon (IX)
relatively prime (VIII)
repeated division (IX)
repeated subtraction (VIII)
repeating decimal (VII)
restriction (IX)
reverse (VIII)
right (circular) cylinder (IX)
right isosceles triangle (IX)
right prism (VII)
right scalene triangle (IX)
right triangle (V)
rigid (IX)
rod (VI)
Roman (numeration) system (IX)
round (-ed)down (IX)
round (-ed, -ing) off (V)
round (-ed) up (IX)

S satisfies (IX)
scale (of a drawing, map, etc.) (IV)
scale drawing (VII)
scalene (triangle) (IX)
scientific notation (VIII)
score (meaning number of years) (IX)
second axis (IX)
second partial product (VIII)
second power (IX)
sector (VII)
segment unit (IX)
semicircle (VIII)
septagon (IX)
septillion (IX)
several (VI)
sextillion (IX)
short division (IX)
short method (VIII)
short vertical form (VIII)
shortcut (short cut) (VI)

EDL Mathematics Core Vocabulary for Grades 1-3 and 4-6

signed whole number (IX)
similar (V)
similar triangles (VIII)
similarity (VIII)
simple closed curve (V)
simple closed figure (VI)
simple closed surface (V)
simpler form (IX)
simplest decimal (numeral) (VIII)
simplest form (II)
simplest fraction (form) (IX)
simplest name (VII)
simplest numeral (III)
simplest terms (IX)
simplify (VI)
skew lines (IX)
skip count, -ing (IX)
solid (IX)
solid figure (IX)
solution pair (IX)
solution set (III)
some-all-no (rule, sentence, statement) (IX)
space figure (VII)
space geometry (IX)
space region (IX)
square centimeter (VII)
square foot (feet) (IV)
square inch (V)
square kilometer (IX)
square meter (VIII)
square mile (VI)
square millimeter (IX)
square number (IX)
square prism (IX)
square pyramid (IX)
square region (VI)
square root (VIII)
square yard (VI)
squared (no other form) (IX)
standard (IX)
standard mixed numeral (form) (VIII)
standard unit (VI)
statute mile (IX)
story problem (VIII)
straight angle (VIII)
straight edge (VIII)

subscript (IX)
substitute (VIII)
subtraction numeral (IX)
subtractive (IX)
successful outcome (IX)
successive outcome (IX)
super set (superset) (VIII)
supplementary angles (VIII)
surface area (V)
symbolism (IX)
symbolize (VIII)
symmetric property (IX)
system (IV)

T tablespoon (IX)
tally mark (IX)
tangent (IX)
teaspoon (IX)
ten millions (VIII)
tens' digit (VIII)
tens' man (men) (T-man) (VIII)
tens' place (column) (VI)
ten thousands (V)
ten thousands' place (IX)
ten thousandth (VIII)
tenths (II)
tenths' place (VIII)
terminate (IX)
terminating decimal (VIII)
terms (of a numeral, etc.) (VI)
tetrahedron (VIII)
theorem of Pythagoras (VIII)
thick, -ness (VI)
thin (IX)
third partial product (IX)
third power (VIII)
thousands' digit (IX)
thousands' period (IX)
thousands' place (VII)
thousandth (V)
thousandths' place (IX)
through (III)

time (interest or rate term) (VII)
ton-mile (IX)
total value (VII)
trace, -d, tracing (V)
transitive property (VIII)
transversal (IX)
trapezoid (VII)
trial (IX)
triangular number (IX)
triangular prism (VIII)
triangular pyramid (IX)
trillion (VIII)
triple, -d (IX)
truncated cone (IX)
twin primes (VIII)
two-stage problem (IX)

U undivided (IX)
union of line segments (IX)
union of sets (VI)
unit of surface (surface unit) (VIII)
unit angle (VIII)
unit fractional number (VII)
unit plane region (IX)
unit region (VIII)
unit segment (IX)
unit square region (IX)
universal set (universe) (VIII)
unlimited (IX)
unmatched (IX)
unnamed addend (VIII)
unnamed minuend (IX)
upper bound (VIII)
upper limit (IX)
upward (IX)

V variable (VII)
vertical angle (VII)
vertical axis (IX)
vertical bar graph (IX)
vertical coordinate (IX)
vertical scale (VIII)
volume measure (VIII)

W weigh (III)

whole-number answer (VIII)
whole-number factor (IX)
word problem (IX)
working form (VII)

X x-axis (IX)

Y yardstick (IX)
year (I)

Z zero numerator (IX)
zero power (IX)

EDL Science Core Vocabulary for Grades 3, 4, 5, and 6

Science 3

A
absorb
accurate
activities
algae
amphibian
ancient
animal
    animal keeper
    animal kingdom
    animal tracks
ant
atmosphere

B
backbone
beak
bilateral
bilateral symmetry
boil

C
calendar
carbon
carbon dioxide
cell
    electric cell
    sperm cell
Celsius
chemical
    chemical energy
chlorine
classify
cloud
coal
community
condense
conductor
contract
coral
    coral reef

D
decay
degree
depend
desert
dismal
dissolve
dry

E
ear
    ear drum
    inner ear
    middle ear
    outer ear
earth
    earthworm
    earth satellite

egg
    egg cell
electric
    electric energy
electricity
energy
    energy of motion
    mechanical energy
    stored energy
environment
equator
evaporate
exercise
expand
extinct

F
fahrenheit
fault
ferns
fertile
fertilizer
flood
force
fossil
fuel
fungus

G
gas
    natural gas
geyser
gills
glacier
gravity

H
heat
hibernate
humus

I
infection
insect
instinct

J
joint

L
larva
lava
leaf
liquid
location
lungs

M
mammal
map
melting
    melting point
messages
meter
mineral
model
molecule
moon
    full moon
    new moon
    moon year
muscle
music

N
nerve
    nerve cord

O
ocean
organ
outlet
ovary

P
phase
    phase change
pistil
planet
plant
    plant kingdom
pollen
    pollen come
    pollen grains
pollute
power
preserved
prove
pupil
pure

R
reflect
reproduce
reptile
rib
root
    root hairs

S
satellite
season
seed
plant seed
    seed coat
    seed cone
seedling
senses

skeleton
skin
snake
sniff
space
spider
spore
    spore case
stamen
star
    star year
steam
stem
stretch
stunts
sundial
surface

T
taste
temperature
    kindling
        temperature
thermometer
thunder
tides
tongue

U
upright

V
vocal
    vocal cords
volcano

W
water
fresh water
salt water
water vapor
wheat

Science 4

A
abdomen
adapt
adaptation
air
    air pressure
alert
amoeba
ancestor
anus
apply
area
astronaut
astronomer

77

atom
axis

B bacteria
balance
battery
behavior
blood vessels
breathe
budding
burning

C calcium
canyon
capillary
carbohydrate
cartilage
cell
    cell division
    cell nucleus
    cell wall
centimeter
change
chemical
    chemical change
    chemical weathering
chemist
chlorophyll
circuit
circulate
circulation
climate
communicate
compound
conduct
constellation
continent
contraction
control
convex
    convex lens
    convex mirror
core
    core sample
cork
crust
current

D density
    population density
diameter
diaphragm
digestion
    digestive juices
dinosaurs
disease

distance
divide
dome

E echo
eclipse
embryo
erosion
esophagus
evaporation
evidence

F fan
fat
filament
flow
food chain
friction
funnel
    funnel cloud

G gravitational
    gravitational
      acceleration
    gravitational
      attraction
    gravitational force

H habitat
    artificial habitat
    natural habitat
hemisphere
horizon
hurricane

I incisor

L leaf
    leaf scar
length
lens
    concave lens
    converging lens
    convex lens
    telephoto lens
    wide angle lens
lever
liquid
    liquid crystal

M mantle
marble
mass
    gross mass
    net mass

mathematics
matter
maximum
measure
measurement
membrane
mercury
metric
    metric system
microscope
molar
mold
moss
motion
mouth

N natural
nervous
nucleus

O orbit
organism
oxygen
    oxygen cycle

P pendulum
period
periodic
physical
    physical change
pitch
planet
plankton
pollutant
pollution
population
predict
produce
producer
protein
protozoan
pulse
    pulse rate
pupa
pupil

Q quarter

R radiant
    radiant energy
    radiant heat
rain
    rain gauge
    rainfall
range

red blood
    red blood cell
    red blood corpuscle
reproduction
response
retina
revolve
ridge

S saliva
salivary
    salivary gland
scale
    scale model
sediment
sedimentary
    sedimentary rock
shape
shift
sight
solid
solution
sound
    sound wave
sperm
    sperm cell
spinal
    spinal column
starch
stethoscope
stimulus
stomach
store
strand
stream
survive
swamp
switch
system

T tendon
tidal
    tidal wave
treatment
tune
turn

U unit

V valley
variable
variation
vein
vibration
vitamin

EDL Science Core Vocabulary for Grades 3, 4, 5, and 6

W
water
  water cycle
  water shed
  water table
wave
weight
wingspread

Science 5

A
accelerate
acid
action
  action—reaction
air
  air foil
  air mass
  air sacs
ammonia
anatomy
aorta
artery
  pulmonary artery
automatic
  automatic behavior
  automatic reflex
average
  average speed

B
bacteriologist
base
biceps
blood
  blood stream
bone
  bone cells
  bone marrow
boulder
brain
  brainstem

C
calcium
  calcium hydroxide
calorie
cell
  cell covering
  dry cell
cerebellum
cerebrum
characteristics
chemical
  chemical reaction
  chemical test
chemically

circulatory
  circulatory system
circumference
cloud
  cirrus clouds
  cumulonimbus
    clouds
  cumulus clouds
cocoon
compass
compound
  compound machine
concave
  concave lens
conduction
connective
  connective tissue
consume
consumer
controlled
  controlled
    experiment
convection
cornea
corrosive
crater
crystal
  crystal faces
cycle

D
data
decompose
decomposer
detect
detector
dew
  dew point
digest
digestive
  digestive system
dissection

E
earth
  earthquake
ecosystem
electric
  electric charge
  electric current
  electric motor
electromagnet
electron
element
elevation
ellipse

energy
  energy cycle
environment
  hostile environment
epicycle
equator
evolve
evolution
excretion
experiment
  controlled
    experiment
experimenter

F
focus
food
  food pyramid
  food web
formula
fossil
  fossil fuels
front
frosted
fuse
fusion

G
galvanometer
generally
generator
geologist
geology
gill
  gill slit
gland
glucose
granite
gravitation
growth
  growth rate

H
hail
hurl
hypothesis

I
igneous
  igneous rock
image
indicator
inertia
insulator
interact
invertebrate

K
kilogram

L
launch
launcher
lens
  lens eyepiece
  lens objective
life
  life function
  life span
light
  light meter
  light year
limestone
limit
  limiting factor
lintel
liver

M
magma
magnet
magnetite
malaria
metamorphic
  metamorphic rock
metamorphosis
meteor
meteorite
meteorologists
model
muscle
  muscle cell
  voluntary muscle

N
nerve
  nerve cell
  nerve impulse
  nerve tissue
  optic nerve
nervous
  nervous system
neutral
nutrient

O
observe
observation
optical
  optical illusion
orbital
  orbital speed
organ
  organ system
organic
oxide
oxidation

79

P pancreas
parallel
   parallel circuit
photosynthesis
physical
   physical property
pigment
plastic
potential
   potential energy
precious
pressure
prism
property
protein

Q quarry

R reaction
   reaction time
reflex
   reflex action
relative
   relative humidity
respiration
respiratory
revolution

S scar
section
sensory
   sensory fiber
   sensory nerve
skeletal
   skeletal system
slant
soil
solar
   solar system
species
stable
structure
subject
substance
survive
tensile
thermostat
thrust
tissues
transfer
   transfer of energy

T tropical

U universe

V valve
vein
   varicose vein
ventricle
vertebra
vertebrate
vocalization
volume

W warm
   warm-blooded
weather

Y yeast
   yeast culture

Science 6

A acid
   amino acid
air
   air bladder
   air resistance
alchemist
alloy
ampere
angle
   angle of incidence
   angle of reflection
annual
antibiotic
aqualung
association
atomic
   atomic number
   atomic pile
   atomic weight

B barometer
battery
bond
brittle
buckle
bulbs

C carbon
   carbon compounds
cell
   cell covering
   connecting nerve cell
   sex cell
   solar cell
   specialized cell
   wet cell

cellulose
chromium
color
   color blind
   color spectrum
combination
comet
complex
compress
compression
concave
   concave mirror
concept
   self-concept
condensation
conservation
convection
   convection currents
corona
crest
cross
   cross-pollinate
current
   current of electricity
cutting
cylinder

D diet
diffuse
diffusion
digestive
   digestive tubes
diverge
dominant

E electric
   electric charge
   electric circuit
   electric impulse
   electric potential
electron
   electron emission
   electron microscope
elliptical
endocrine
energy
   nuclear energy
enzyme

F fission
fixed (as in space)
fleece
fluid
frequency
fulcrum

G galaxy
galvanometer
gene

H hazardous
heat
   heat of fusion
   heat of vaporization
   heat capacity
   heat energy
   heat waves
humidity
   relative humidity

I image
   real image
   virtual image
infrared
   infrared radiation
   infrared waves
inherit
instinctively
insulator
intestine
   large intestine
   small intestine

K kilowatt
   kilowatt hour
kinetic
   kinetic energy

L life
   life cycle
line
   line of sight
lines of force
   lines of incidence
   line's of reflection

M magnetic
   magnetic field
marine
mature
maturity
microorganism
molting
motor
motor nerve cells
motor nerves
mutant
mutation

EDL Science Core Vocabulary for Grades 3, 4, 5, and 6

N nerve
    connecting nerve
    motor nerve
    nerve ending
    nerve fiber
neutron
nitrate
nitrogen
nodules
nuclear
    nuclear energy
    nuclear reaction
    nuclear reactor

O orb-web
ore
overpopulation

P palps
permanent
physical
    physical tolerance
plot (as in navigate)
pollinate
positive
predator
prey
primitive
privacy
process
proton
pulley
    fixed pulley
    movable pulley

R radio
    radio transmitter
    radio waves
    radioactive
ray
rayon
reaction
    chain reaction
    chemical reaction
    combination reaction
reason
refraction
release
resistant

S seep
sensory
    sensory neurons
similar

simple
    simple reflexes
    simple machine
slope
smog
solar
    solar cell
    solar eclipse
    solar energy
    solar flare
specific
spectrum
state
static
    static electricity
stress

T telescope
tissues
tornado
translucent
transparent
trough
turbine

U ultraviolet
    ultraviolet radiation
urban

V vacuum
vary
vibrate

W wave
    wavelength
    wave theory
wedge

Y yolk

——— EDL Social Studies Core Vocabulary for Grades 3, 4, 5, and 6 ———

Social Studies 3

A
acre
ancestor
arctic
automobile

B
bar
budget
business

C
cacao
canal
capital
  capital goods
central
chief
  chief executive
city
  city council
  city hall
  city manager
  city ordinance
  city planner
  city services
climate
coast
colonist
colony
common
community
compass
Congress
constitution
continent
continental
conveyor
country
county
court
crops
cross
cultural
culture

D
dam
declaration
degrees
  degrees of
    temperature
department
desert
direct
direction

E
earthquake
  earthquake zone
East
elect
environment
equator
explain
explore
explorer

F
fact
factory
fort
freedom
fresh
frontier

G
glacier
global
globe
goods
government
grassland
group

H
harbor
harvest
hinterlands
holiday

I
immigrant
industry
inspect
invent
invention
iron
  iron ore
island

J
judge

L
law
  lawmakers

M
mainland
manager
map
  map key
  maps and globes
market
mayor
metropolitan
migrant

model
mountain

N
nation
nationality
natural
neighborbood
nomad

O
ocean

P
peninsula
physical
plain
planet
plantation
plateau
pole
  North Pole
  South Pole
pollution
power
precipitation
president
property
public

R
rapids
raw
region
represent
representative
residential
revolution
route
rule
rural
rush

S
scale
season
separation
service
settlement
share
slave
  slave trade
slum
spirit
suburb
suburban
surface

T
tax
taxation
telegraph
textile
tide

town
  town board
trade
traffic
transportation

U

V
valley
village

W
wage
warehouse
weather
wholesale

Z
zone

Social Studies 4

A
aborigines
accent
adobe
agricultural
agriculture
air
alphabet
altitude
amendment
anthropologist
anthropology
area
assembly
atmosphere
attitude
automatic
automation

B
balance
banded
barter
basic
bay
belt

C
canyons
carnival
caste
cavalrymen
cereal
chutes
civil
communicate
competition
conservation
constitutional
consumer
consumption

contour
cooperation
coral
corral
cotton
council
credit
current
custom

D
delta
demand
democracy
depression
develop
development
diet
dike
distance
division
drought

E
economic
economist
economy
education
efficient
empire
energy
equatorial

F
famine
favored
features
federal
fertilizer
fiber
flint
foreign
foreigner
fossil
frontier

G
generator
geography
gin
global
grain
grid
grindstones
guide

H
habit
harvest
hazy
hemisphere
history
hollow
humus

EDL Social Studies Core Vocabulary for Grades 3, 4, 5, and 6

I
igloo
independence
independent
industrial
information
institution
intensive
interchangeable
interview
inventor
investment
irrigate
irrigation

J jungle

K
kayak
kilometer

L
labor
language
latitude
legend
level
line
loom

M
machete
material
mechanize
meridians
mesa
meters
migration
mineral
minority
modern
moisture
monsoon

N
native
needs
neighboring

O
oasis
overpopulation
oxygen

P
paddy
palm
partnership
pioneer
polar

political
population
primary
prime
produce
production
profit
progressive

R
range
relief
religion
religious
republic
reservation
reservoir
resources
role
rugged
ruins

S
sacred
sari
science
scientific
scientist
sea
secondary
servant
settle
sharecropper
shelter
shock
skill
social
sociologist
sociology
sod
soil
solar
specialization
square
subcontinent
supply
swamp
symbol
system

T
taro
technology
telescope
temperature
temple
territories
thresh
topsoil
traditional
trap
treaty

tribe
tropic

U
union
untouchable
urban
urge

V
vegetation
volcano

W winnow

Social Studies-5

A
abolitionism
abolitionist
adapt
advertise
agent
alliance
anvil
appeal
apprentice
archaeologist
archaeology
architecture
armor
art
assemble
authority

B
barbarian
basin
bazaar
behavior
boycott
bureau
burgesses

C
cabinet
cape
captivity
caravan
census
century
ceremony
choice
Christian
civilization
civilized
clan
classical
cluster
code
commonwealth
complex
compromise

consent
contract
control
convention
countdown
craft
crater
crusades

D
decision
density
descendant
dictatorship
disaster
disciple
discipline
disposable
distribute
distribution
divide
domestic
domesticated

E
ecology
ecological
elevation
emancipation
emperor
equipment
executive
exile
exploration
export
extend

F
feast
federalism
federation
fertile
fiord
fragrant
frontierism

G
generation
glide
governor
graph
guerrilla

H
hacienda
hardship
haul
heaven
historical
holy
homesteader
hub

I
iceberg
immigration
import
inaugurate
inauguration
indentured
intelligence
interpret

J
journal
journey
Judaism
judicial
jury

L
legislative
legislator
levee
liberty
limit
longhouse
longitude
loyalist

M
maize
manor
manufacture
manufacturer
marksman
mass
megalopolis
migrate
military
minstrel
mission
missionary
monarchy
monk
monopoly
monotheism
monotheist
mosque
mound
Muslim

N
nature
neutral
noble

O
official
organization
organize

P
pampas
parallel
parka
parliament
passage
patriot

83

EDL Social Studies Core Vocabulary for Grades 3, 4, 5, and 6

patriotic
patriotism
peak
peasant
permanent
persecute
persecution
petition
philosopher
philosophy
politics
pollute
polytheism
polytheist
popular
priest
proclamation
producer
product
projection
prophecy
prophet
protectorate
province
pulp

R radical
ram
reference
reform
refugee
region
relationship
repair
responsibility
revenge
revolt

S sacrifice
sap
secede
segregate
segregation
sharecropping
silt
sin
society
source
stain
state
steppe
stock
strait
strike
subsist

subsistence
supernatural
supreme
surplus
synagogue

T thatch
timber
tortilla
tourist
tournament
trait
traitor
transport
tributary
tribute
tropical
tundra
tyranny
tyrant

U underground
V value
venture
voyage
W war
warfare
wilderness
worship

Social Studies 6

A abdicate
absolute
afterlife
ally
Anglo-American
aristocracy
aristocrat
artifact
astronomy
auction

B belch
beliefs
biological
biology
bishop
Buddhism
bureaucracy
burgher

C capitalism
capitalist
Catholic
character

charter
Christianity
city-state
colonization
colonize
command
commission
communication
communism
conquer
craftsmen
creole
crisis
cultivation
cuneiform
cycle

D data
delegate
democratic
deposit
dictator
diplomat
dominance
dominant
dynasty

E encomienda
environmental
evidence
exchange
extreme

F federalism
feudal
feudalism
foundation
frequency

G growth
H hare
heretic
heritage
hidalgo
Hinduism
human
humanism
humanitarianism
humid
hypothesis

I ideal
imperialism
industrialization
industrialize
interest
interior
invest

J joint
jury

L linguist
literature
luxury

M marine
mature
medieval
mediterranean
mestizos
middle
miniature
monarch
moral
mount
movement
myth

N nationalism
nationalization
nationalize
naturalize
navigation
nobel
nuclear

O opium
optic
oracle
oral

P patron
patronage
permanent
perspective
pharaoh
pope
possession
prehistoric
prehistory
prevailing
priest
prosperous
protest
psychological
psychologist
puritan
pyramid

R rank
reef
Reformation
Renaissance
republican
resist
respond
ritual

S savanna
scribe
serf
serfdom
shogun
slavery
socialism
species
sphere
standard
steppe
stirring
stockbroker
subsistence

T theory
tierra
tilt
tissue
trade

V vassal
vast
vehicle
vernacular
veto
viceroy

Appendix:

Origin and Organization of the Vocabulary Lists

READING CORE VOCABULARY

Background

The purpose underlying the preparation of the Basic Vocabulary was to establish a core vocabulary for the various materials in the EDL language arts program. It is the authors' belief that any well-integrated language arts program should maintain vocabulary controls that make possible short-interval learning with enough repetition and reinforcement so that each student will be assured of a minimum level of language development as he progresses from level to level. As a result of this thinking, a core vocabulary list was formulated which incorporated those words judged to be most fundamental to communication based on studies and evaluations of basal reading series, other widely approved vocabulary

studies, and other frequently employed vocabulary-building instructional materials.

Primarily, this word list will be used in the preparation of basic and supplementary instructional materials in printed or projected form for use in EDL language arts programs. Materials prepared from this list would serve to introduce and reinforce a minimum language requirement, but would also contain a planned amount of above-level, specific-area reading and enrichment to provide for continuing vocabulary development.

Secondly, this list can serve as a continuous instructional guide for the classroom teacher, providing her with a constant check as to words which pupils should have learned at previous levels. If the teacher ensures mastery of the basic vocabulary required at each level, she knows that each pupil has the essential language foundation from which to extend his vocabulary.

Thirdly, there is a constant demand for graded materials designed for independent reading by pupils on primary and intermediate levels. The vocabulary load of such material should, of course, be carefully controlled. Authors who wish to prepare graded reading material for use by EDL or by other publishers will find this list an invaluable aid.

Further, this list may eventually serve as the basis for those portions of readability scales that are concerned with an appraisal of vocabulary difficulty.

BACKGROUND OF THE STUDY

Vocabulary study at EDL began in 1949, when an attempt was made to arrive at a minimum vocabulary for reading, writing, and speaking that would be acceptable by each state in the Union. Over 150 sources were checked during the initial study, and the resulting graded word list contained the 6,310 words judged to be most important for children in grades one to eight.[1] Revisions of this list were published in 1951[2] and 1955.[3]

While this list proved satisfactory as a general vocabulary guide, more rigid controls were indicated when reading materials were to be prepared for use in the primary and intermediate grades. As a consequence, an additional study of nine basal reading series was undertaken in 1968 with the express purpose of determining the grade point at which the required words for grades 1-6 and their variant forms should be introduced. The series studied were those published by:

Allyn and Bacon, Inc.
American Book Company
Ginn and Company
Harper & Row
Holt, Rinehart and Winston
Houghton Mifflin Company
Lyons and Carnahan, Inc.
The Macmillan Company
Scott, Foresman and Company

At present, it is the authors' conviction that one common list can and should serve as a base for all language arts instruction. Further, the fact that the student's first encounter with words in visual form is through reading indicates that reading level should be the primary factor in deciding on the grade placement of words. The same words can be and at present are generally re-introduced in the following grade for spelling and writing activities. This amount of lag between reading and spelling levels was determined by comparing the grade placement of words in a number of widely used spelling lists with grade placement of the same words in reading series.[4]

Because reading level was to be the major consideration in determining grade placement, the decision was made to use the basal reading series as a source on all levels for which published lists are available. This approach was judged to be essential at the primary level. At the intermediate level, where there is more divergence in the words introduced, the findings of the most authoritative studies of usage by pupils and frequency of occurrence in reading material were used as additional controls in selecting words.

PROCEDURE USED IN COMPILING THE WORD LISTS

Grades 1-8

The procedure followed in compiling the word lists was similar to that advocated by Buckingham and Dolch[5] in that the amount of word load was first determined for each grade, and then a decision was made as to the types of words to be included. Following this, procedures and sources for the selection of words were established.

1. Word Load

The first step in determining the word load per grade was to consult the basal readers and find the average number of words introduced at each level. No two series use exactly the same vocabulary, nor do they use the same number of words at any given level. Of the nine basal reading series, the average number of words introduced at each grade level is:

P	1	2	3	4	5	6
68	273	440	708	787	1,063	1,077

Although these figures were used as a base, the

---

[1] Stanford E. Taylor, *Basic Vocabulary*. New York: Washington Square Reading Center, 1949.

[2] Earl A. Taylor, Stanford E. Taylor, and Helen Frackenpohl, *Basic Vocabulary* (Second Edition). Levittown, New York: Educational Development Laboratories, Inc. 1951.

[3] Stanford E. Taylor and Helen Frackenpohl, *Basic Vocabulary* (Third Revision). Huntington, New York: Educational Development Laboratories, Inc., 1955.

[4] This lag represents an overall average. In any spelling series, the words selected for a given grade include a great number of words not yet introduced in reading as well as a number of words that may have been introduced in reading a number of grades earlier. One of the reasons for this variation appears to be concern with the words' structure or form and with only a general consideration with word meaning as it relates to reading.

[5] B. R. Buckingham and E. W. Dolch, *A Combined Word List*. Boston: Ginn and Company, 1936.

word load was increased in certain grades where it was judged possible to successfully teach a greater number of basic words by more advanced instructional means. This is especially true of the intermediate levels. In addition, the trend reflected by the survey of the basal series seems to be toward increased word load on these levels.

The final word count for each grade level is as follows:

P	1	2	3	4	5	6	7	8	Total
68	311	527	850	992	1,201	1,378	802	862	6,991

2. Types of Words Included

In an attempt to include the most commonly used words in American English, words were selected which have general, specific, technical (if widely used), and social significance. Although root words have been stressed, in some instances it seemed desirable to include derived forms (especially in the lower grades). Proper names were avoided for the most part, but names of the days of the week, months, and widely observed holidays were included. Also included were the more common contractions and abbreviations. Most sound words, such as "meow" and "moo," and movement words, such as "hippety" and "zoom," were omitted. Provincialisms and colloquialisms were also omitted. Moreover, no attempt was made to include the more technical vocabularies for specific subjects and areas of learning.

3. Procedure for the Selection of Words

Grades 1-3

The lists for grade levels 1-3 were determined by the point of introduction in the nine basal series listed earlier. The frequency point at which a word was added to the list was set at 3 out of 9. (When a higher frequency was used, the desired word load could not be achieved, and the level of difficulty of the vocabulary was reduced considerably.)

Grades 4-6

The words for these levels were selected from the following sources:

A Basic Vocabulary of Elementary School Children, by Henry D. Rinsland.[1]

The Teacher's Word Book of 30,000 Words, by Edward L. Thorndike and Irving Lorge.[2]

Those basal reading series which provide alphabetical lists of words introduced are:

Sheldon Basic Reading Series (Allyn and Bacon, Inc.)

Betts Basic Readers, Third Edition (American Book Company)

The Ginn Basic Readers, Ginn 100 Edition (Ginn and Company)

The Harper & Row Basic Reading Program (Harper & Row)

Winston Basic Readers (Holt, Rinehart and Winston)

Reading for Meaning (Houghton Mifflin Company)

The Development Reading Series (Lyons and Carnahan)

The Macmillan Reading Program (The Macmillan Company)

The New Basic Readers (Scott, Foresman and Company)

Words occurring in at least three basals on the same level or below were judged to be suitable for that level. Words occurring twice at the same level or below were checked first against the Rinsland list to confirm student knowledge of the word at that level and next against the Thorndike-Lorge list to determine whether a word was used frequently enough in written material (G listing) to justify its inclusion. In using the Thorndike-Lorge list, the authors' recommendations were used with regard to qualifying frequency. In some instances where questions arose regarding inclusion of a specific word, the Iowa Spelling Scale[3] was consulted.

Grades 7-8

The vocabularies of the various basal readers on this level are so divergent that they are no longer of great importance as a vocabulary control. At these levels, the balance of the words suggested by the basals in grades 4 to 6 and not yet included in the vocabulary list (on the basis of too low a frequency) were rechecked against the Rinsland and Thorndike-Lorge lists and added to the list if their frequencies then warranted. The remainder of the word load for these two levels was derived almost exclusively from the Rinsland and the Thorndike-Lorge lists, using the same general approach as previously described.

It will be noticed that in the Revised Core Vocabulary, the word load on levels 7 and 8 is lower than in the previous edition. The changes in word load for these two grades now reflect downgrading of vocabulary as a result of the 1968 survey of basals for grades 1-6.

Grades 9-13

Between the words taught through eighth grade and those that are infrequently used and rather obscure

---

[1] Published by the University of Oklahoma, 1945.

[2] Published by the Bureau of Publications, Teachers College, Columbia, 1944.

[3] Harry A. Greene, *The New Iowa Spelling Scale.* Iowa City, Iowa: State University of Iowa, Bureau of Educational Research and Service, (undated).

in nature lie approximately 2,000 words (of the types previously described). The word loads for grades 9, 10, 11, and 12 were set at approximately 500 per grade level. This amount of words represents a feasible number for instruction over a year's time. The number of words for grade 13 was reduced to approximately 400 because of the greater difficulty of words on this level. The actual word load figures after the completion of the list are as follows:

9	10	11	12	13	Total
420	477	542	540	432	2,411

Selecting words for these levels is at best a highly subjective task. Seemingly the only guides that can be used are the Thorndike-Lorge list and the various vocabulary improvement materials in wide use on these levels. In using the Thorndike-Lorge list, the highest frequency words, ranging from the more to the less frequently used, were selected. Modifications (upgrading and downgrading) and additions were made according to frequency of occurrence of words in the vocabulary improvement materials (see bibliography).

MATHEMATICS CORE VOCABULARY

Background

The use of vocabulary lists to indicate concept load for some particular content area dates back to fifteenth-century England when lists of words with their frequencies were compiled for use by shorthand writers.[1] In this country, the first lists compiled for pedagogical purposes were for the content areas of spelling (Ayres) and reading (Thorndike).[2] The works of Horn and Dolch, and Taylor, Frackenpohl, and White have updated the vocabulary lists for these content areas.[3]

In the area of vocabulary lists for mathematics (arithmetic), the single most significant work was done by Luella Cole in 1942. She compiled previous vocabulary studies of technical terms in mathematics (arithmetic) into a total of 224 words, 194 of which were classified as being pertinent to the elementary mathematics curriculum. Geometry words which now appear as early as first grade in modern

mathematics series were listed separately in her study under the content area of geometry. Although the terms on Cole's list were given a Thorndike rating for frequency, she cautioned that high frequency in general reading matter did not necessarily help students to understand a word's highly technical meaning in the content area of instructional materials.[4]

Even though later studies by Repp, Kerfoot, Stauffer, and Shaw have pointed to discrepancies in the introduction and continuity of usage of mathematical terminology in certain modern mathematics texts, there continues to be a need for a core listing of modern mathematical terms used in modern mathematics texts today.[5]

While no tabulation of mathematical terms can be considered final, this *Core Vocabulary for Mathematics, Grades 1-6* will provide the teacher, the writer of instructional materials, and the researcher with a valuable source of information on the special vocabulary used in mathematics programs for the elementary grades.

Further delineation of the mathmatical terminology through the use of the frequency concept will provide the reader with information concerning the relative usage of the mathematical terms in representative basal modern mathematics text currently in use in public elementary schools. Terms judged to be of high importance but found to have a low frequency in instructional materials should be given additional instructional time for learning and reinforcement.

PURPOSE OF, AND NEED FOR, THE STUDY

The purpose of this study was to compile an inventory of the usage and frequency of modern mathematical terms in commonly-used basal mathematics series in the public schools, for elementary grades one through six. The information compiled in this *Core Vocabulary for Mathematics, Grades 1-6* represents the combination of two studies: one by Willmon on the usage and frequency of mathematical terms in the primary grade modern math texts, and

[1] Charles C. Fries and A. Aileen Traver, *English Word Lists*. Ann Arbor, Michigan: The George Wahr Publishing Company, 1965, p. 2.
[2] Leonard P. Ayres, *A Measuring Scale for Ability in Spelling* New York: The Russell Sage Foundation, 1915; Edward L. Thorndike, *The Teacher's Wordbook of 10,000 Words*. New York: Bureau of Publications, Columbia University, 1921.
[3] Earnest A. Horn, *A Basic Writing Vocabulary*. Iowa City, Iowa: College of Education, 1923; Edward W. Dolch, "The Use of Vocabulary Lists in Predicting Readability and in Developing Reading Materials," *Elementary English,* vol. 26 (March 1949), pp. 142-149; Stanford E. Taylor, Helen Frackenpohl, and Catherine E. White, *A Revised Core Vocabulary*. New York: Educational Developmental Laboratories, A Division of McGraw-Hill Book Company, 1969.
[4] Luella Cole, *The Teacher's Handbook of Technical Vocabulary*. Bloomington, Illinois: Public School Publishing Company, 1940, pp. 25-26.
[5] Florence C. Repp, "The Vocabularies of Five Recent Third Grade Arithmetic Textbooks," *Arithmetic Teacher,* vol. 7 March 1960, pp. 128-132; James F. Kerfoot, "The Vocabulary in Primary Arithmetic Texts," *The Reading Teacher,* vol. 14 January 1961, pp. 177-180; Russell G. Stauffer "A Vocabulary Study Comparing Arithmetic, Health, and Science Texts," *The Reading Teacher,* vol. 30 November 1966, pp. 141-147; U.S. Office of Education, *Reading Problems in Mathematics,* by Judith Shaw, ED 016 587, Bethesda, Maryland: ERIC Document Reproduction Service, 1967, pp. 5-11.

the second by Browning on the usage and frequency of mathematical terms in the intermediate grade texts.[1]

A review of the research literature made by Willmon[2] indicates that many learning problems in mathematics are caused by reading difficulties.[3]

Readability studies of math textbooks specifically suggest that the technical vocabulary load may be the source of the major reading difficulties.[4] These findings are supported by research in the general area of readability where it has been found that vocabulary influences the comprehension difficulty level of instructional materials, with the difficulty level increasing in the content area of instructional materials.[5] Because the vocabulary load of a content area does represent for the student the most significant portion of the reading done in that subject area, a need is indicated for a vocabulary list of technical terms currently used in modern mathematics texts.

The results of this study will provide the mathematics teacher with the terminology used in instructional materials and a knowledge of the words considered most important in terms of frequency.

For example, a working knowledge of the core vocabulary will enable a teacher to see that if a term is of high importance but shows low frequency, it will require more instructional time and material for some students. Terms of infrequent usage and less importance may receive less instructional attention.

It is hoped that teachers, as well as authors of instructional materials, may use the *Core Vocabulary for Mathematics, Grades 1-6* as a basis for updating and/or revising instructional materials in the area of modern mathematics.

PROCEDURE FOR TABULATING PRIMARY TERMS

A total of eight basal arithmetic series were used in the primary word count. First-, second-, and third-grade texts in each of the eight series were included totaling twenty-four books. The following series were used in the word count: Addison Wesley (1968); Houghton Mifflin (1967); Harcourt Brace World (1966-1968); American Book Co. (1968); Singer (1966-1969); Holt, Rinehart and Winston (1966-1968); Laidlaw (1968); Silver Burdett (1968). Texts were selected on the recommendations of professors of mathematics education and of state mathematics supervisors. The chosen series are typical of the most widely used textbooks in public school systems today.

The study was conducted in two phases. In the first phase each page of each text was surveyed and the different specialized words and phrases were listed. This was done in accordance with Travers' recommendations for word-frequency counts.[6] All words, including any general words which become technical when used in the specialized context of mathematics, were included on the list. For example, the words *line* and *point* have a general meaning as well as special mathematics concept.

Twenty-four different texts were examined in order to obtain a wide selection from the vocabularies of various authors. Again, in accordance with recommendations for word counts, graded texts were selected for counting where the content was presented in an organized, sequential form. After the survey, math educators were asked to review the terms and phrases to insure consistency between the reading specialist's point of view and the mathematics specialist's view. After the list was surveyed, a code number was assigned to each word.

The second phase of the study was the frequency count. The word frequency count was done by thirty pairs of counters, one checking on the other. As words were counted, they were recorded on the data sheet. A data sheet was provided for each page in all texts, and if no designated technical words appeared on a page, this was noted.

The following categories were used for definition of items:

Subject or Content-Area Words: Words used to convey concepts and meanings in a particular subject area, such as arithmetic.

Specialized Words: Words denoting a special meaning when used within a particular subject area.

[1] Betty Jean Willmon, "A New Math Terminology List for the Primary Grades: An Instructional Reading Aid," unpublished, Florida State University, 1969; Carole L. Browning, "An Investigation of Selected Mathematical Terminology Found in Five Series of Modern Mathematics Texts for Grades Four, Five and Six," unpublished doctoral dissertation, Florida State University, 1970.

[2] Betty Jean Willmon, "The Importance of Updating Word Lists to Meet Curriculum Needs as Indicated by a Word Frequency Count in One Changing Content Area," paper presented at International Reading Association's Atlantic City convention (in press).

[3] Edwin Eagle, "The Relationship of Certain Reading Abilities to Success in Mathematics," *The Mathematics Teacher,* XLI April 1948, H. C. Johnson, "The Effect of Instruction in Mathematical Vocabulary upon Problem Solving in Arithmetic," *Journal of Educational Research,* XXXVIII, March 1945, George Streby, "Reading in Mathematics," *Arithmetic Teacher,* IV March 1957.

[4] J. K. Smith and J. W. Heddens, "The Readability of Experimental Mathematics Materials," *The Arithmetic Teacher,* XI October 1964; Donovan Johnson. "The Readability of Mathematics Textbooks," *The Mathematics Teacher,* L February 1957; Robert Kane, "The Readability of Mathematics Textbooks," paper presented at National Council of Teachers of Mathematics, Milwaukee, 1969.

[5] Edmund J. Faison, "Readability of Children's Textbooks," *Journal of Educational Psychology,* vol. 42 January 1951; Jeanne Chall, "The Measurement of Readability," *Report of the Tenth Annual Conference on Reading,* ed. Gerald A. Yoakum Pittsburgh Press, 1954.

[6] Robert Travers, *An Introduction to Educational Research.* New York: The Macmillan Company, 1964.

Different Words: A term referring to the procedure of counting each word that is not like another word.

Running Words: A term referring to the procedure of counting all words, one after another, in a text.

Procedures for Word Derivations: Derivations were based on Webster's Seventh New Collegiate Dictionary (1965). Words with such endings as -s, -es, -ies, -ed, and -ing were not counted separately. For the purpose of this study, words with the suffixes -al, -er, -est, -ment, etc., were generally not counted separately. In some limited cases, if the concept of the word was changed radically by adding a

suffix ending, it was then counted separately For example, the terms *addition, subtraction division,* and *multiplication* were counted separately, as the suffix *-ion* gives each a mathematical connotation distinct from the root word.

A tabulation was made for each coded word at each grade level, for each series, and for all series combined. From this tabulation a master comprehensive total was made of the word frequencies.[1]

Based on the frequency of each word, a master list containing a total of 473 words was compiled. Frequencies of the words ranged from 5,995 occurrences down to 1 occurrence. The following table (Table I) is a listing of the frequency categories used in tabulating the words and the number of words that appear in each category.

TABLE I
FREQUENCIES OF PRIMARY ARITHMETIC TERMS

Categories	Frequencies of Usage	Number of Terms
Category I	1,000 +	17
Category II	500–999	27
Category III	100–499	122
Category IV	50–99	58
Category V	35–49	38
Category VI	25–34	39
Category VII	Less than 25	172
	Total	473

PROCEDURE FOR TABULATING INTERMEDIATE TERMS

In order that the list of terminology in the intermediate grade study not become unwieldy, the number of modern mathematics texts examined was reduced to five series, with a total of fifteen texts. On the basis of the results of a twenty-six-state survey of state mathematics supervisors concerning the mathematics texts most popularly used in their respective states for Grades 4, 5, and 6, the modern mathematics series of the following publishers were selected for inclusion in the intermediate-grade inventory:

Addison Wesley (1968)
American Book Company (1968)
Holt, Rinehart and Winston (Nichols and other series, 1968)

Houghton Mifflin (1967)
Laidlaw (1968)

Each of the fifteen texts for Grades 4, 5 and 6 were analyzed for occurrence and frequency of some 743 mathematical terms found in the intermediate-grade texts which had not been analyzed for occurrence and frequency in the primary-grade study by Willmon.

In order to evenly distribute the effects of fatigue from counting words, the fifteen texts were divided into one hundred eleven blocks of approximately fifty pages each. Blocks included only the pages from the text proper and did not include glossaries, the tables of contents, etc. Each fifty-page block was inventoried in a random-order sequence for mathematical terminology found on the intermediate list of terms. The sequence for counting each block was determined by obtaining one random permutation of the numbers from one through one hundred eleven.[2]

---

[1] Betty Willmon, "Reading in the Content Area: A New Math Terminology List for the Primary Grades," *Elementary English,* L (May 1971).

[2] The random sequence used by the researcher for analyzing the fifty-page blocks from the math texts was determined by requesting one random permutation from the APL/1500 programming language, using the form 111?111 on the IBM 1500 Instructional System at the Florida State University Computer Assisted Instruction Center, Tallahassee, Florida, 1970.

The intermediate list of mathematical terms beyond the terms on the Willmon Primary List was used in making the inventory of the intermediate grade texts. As each fifty-page block was counted, terms which appeared from the intermediate list were tallied on a separate tally sheet. Terms were counted only when used with a mathematical meaning; e.g., the word *principal* was counted only when used to mean "a bank-interest term"; when used in other meanings, it was not tallied.

A tabulation of the frequencies of each term was compiled for each of the fifteen texts. From these fifteen tabulations, a master comprehensive inventory of mathematical terminology and their frequencies in the five series was compiled and analyzed.

The following table (Table II) is a listing of the frequency categories used for the tabulation of the mathematical terminology and the number of words that appear in each category:

TABLE II
FREQUENCIES OF INTERMEDIATE ARITHMETIC TERMS

Categories	Frequencies of Usage	Number of Terms
Category I	451 or More	11
Category II	351–450	4
Category III	251–350	6
Category IV	151–250	27
Category V	101–150	26
Category VI	51–100	69
Category VII	26–50	103
Category VIII	11–25	144
Category IX	Less than 10	353
	Total	743

The following restrictions were imposed in counting and tabulating the terms:

1. No terms from the Primary List of Mathematical Terms *were* tabulated.
2. Unless a different form of a term carried a distinct mathematical connotation, all forms of a term *were* counted as the main-entry term. This included (1) plurals; (2) past tenses; (3) comparative and superlative forms of adjectives and adverbs, such as *light, lighter,* and *lightest;* (4) verb forms ending in *-ing, -d,* and *-ed;* and (5) adverbs which were formed by adding *-ly,* such as *exactly.*
3. This list of the 743 terms tabulated includes some terms in parentheses, for example, *if-then (rule, sentence, statement).* This indicates that the *if-then rule, if-then sentence,* and *if-then statement* were *all* tabulated as this entry term.
4. Whenever a term was tabulated for only a specific meaning, it is listed in parentheses; for example, *base (of a figure)* indicates that the term was tabulated only when used in that particular meaning.
5. Title pages, tables of contents, tables of weights, glossaries, etc., *were not* included in the tabulation.
6. All spelled-out terms on the list *were* tabulated.

7. No symbols, numerals, abbreviations, signs, or other characters *were* tabulated.
8. Terms occurring in page headings, topical entries, tables, and pictorial information *were* tabulated.
9. Hyphenated forms of nouns which changed them to modifiers *were not* tabulated.
10. Spelled-out forms of numerals and/or fractions *were not* tabulated.
11. Terms which occurred as a part of the ongoing format of almost every page (or many pages) of the text(s) *were not* tabulated.
12. A term in the list followed in parentheses by *no other form,* such as the term *closed,* means that only that form of the term was tabulated.
13. The plural form of a term is listed in the table if it was more commonly used in the text(s), for example, *corresponding sides.*

SUMMARY AND IMPLICATIONS
An analysis of the mathematics core vocabulary, grades 1 through 6, indicates a heavy vocabulary burden, which suggests a significant obstacle to achievement in mathematics. A review of the technical terms introduced in grades 1, 2, and 3 shows

that only seventeen of the 473 terms are repeated more than one thousand times; most of the technical terms are repeated less than 25 times.[1]

A review of the technical terms introduced in grades 4, 5, and 6 shows that only eleven of the 743 terms are repeated more than 451 times and that 353 (48 percent) of the terms have a frequency of ten or less. Of the total terms, only ten (1.35 percent) were common to all fifteen texts. These ten terms (and their categories of frequency) are as follows: *average* (Category I), *denominator* (Category I), *least* (Category IV), *mixed numeral* Category III), *month* (Category IV), *numerator* (Category III), *per* (Category I), *through* (Category III), *weigh* (Category III), and *year* (Category I). Of the eleven terms appearing in the highest category of frequency, only four were common to all fifteen texts: *denominator, average, year,* and *per.*

In each of the five series of texts, over half of the mathematical terms tabulated had frequencies of ten or less. In two of the series, more than 65 percent of the terms tabulated had frequencies of ten or less. (The reader should keep in mind that a *series frequency* means the frequency of a term *totaled from the three texts of a series;* in other words, 65 percent of the terms had a frequency of ten or less, distributed across the texts composing a series.[2])

The implications for the classroom teacher of the word frequency count of the core vocabulary for modern mathematics are that the technical vocabulary is large, and that the frequency of repetition is inadequate for developing a successful reading vocabulary for mathematics study. Of the terms on the basic primary word list, only 218 of the total 473 terms appear in EDL's *A Revised Core Vocabulary,* and 148 appear in Thorndike's *The Teacher's Wordbook of 10,000 Words.* These findings support the results of the Austin survey that the basal reader approach, as predominantly used, offers limited instruction in content area reading.[3] Therefore, supplementary teaching of vocabulary in mathematics is imperative for developing content area reading skills in mathematics.

Suggestions for the classroom teacher: It is suggested that the *Core Vocabulary for Modern Mathematics, Grades 1-6* be used by classroom teachers:

1. to diagnose for word-knowledge deficiencies related to previously taught mathematics concepts;

2. to inventory a list of terms to be introduced with mathematics topics currently being studied;
3. to organize a list of terms within the different areas of mathematics study (geometry, numeration, operations, sets, and so forth) for sequential reference study;
4. to develop word games, vocabulary activities, dictionaries, story problems, and other supplementary reading aids.

SCIENCE AND SOCIAL STUDIES CORE VOCABULARIES

In late 1977 EDL began planning a vocabulary series to help students learn the meanings of words used in the science and social studies curricula. Students typically have difficulty in science and social studies classes because they do not know or understand the meanings of the concept-bearing words used in these classes.

To determine which concept words were presented and at what level they were introduced, the glossaries of science and social studies series of the following publishers were consulted:

Science Series	Social Studies Series
Addison Wesley	Addison Wesley
American Book Company	Allyn and Bacon
Ginn and Company	American Book Company
Harcourt Brace Jovanovich	Benefic Press
Holt, Rinehart, and Winston	Ginn and Company
Laidlaw Brothers	Harcourt Brace Jovanovich
J. B. Lippincott	Holt, Rinehart, and Winston
Silver Burdett	Houghton Mifflin
Webster/McGraw-Hill	Macmillan

Two criteria were used for placing a word at a given grade level: If a word appeared three or more times in glossaries at a given level, it was placed on the list for that level. If a word appeared less than three times but did appear in the Reading Core Vocabulary at that grade level, it was placed on the list for that level.

[1] Willmon, "Reading in the Content Area."
[2] Browning, "An Investigation of Selected Mathematical Terminology."
[3] Mary Austin, *The Torch Lighters,* Cambridge: Harvard University Press, 1961.